MW00653432

SAINTS FOR YOUNG CHRISTIANS

S A I N T S

FOR YOUNG CHRISTIANS

Written and illustrated by
DAVID R. PREVITALI

A L B A · H O U S E   NEW · YORK

SOCIETY OF ST. PAUL, 2187 VICTORY BLVD., STATEN ISLAND, NEW YORK 10314

Library of Congress Cataloging-in-Publication Data

Previtali, David.
    Saints for young Christians / David R. Previtali.
        p.   cm.
    ISBN 0-8189-0666-9
    1. Christian saints — Biography.   I. Title.
    BX44655.2.P75   1996
    282'.092'2 — dc20   96-8390
        [B]   CIP

Produced and designed in the United States of America by the
Fathers and Brothers of the Society of St. Paul,
2187 Victory Boulevard, Staten Island, New York 10314,
as part of their communications apostolate.

ISBN: 0-8189-0666-9

Printing Information:

Current Printing - first digit	1	2	3	4	5	6	7	8	9	10

Year of Current Printing - first year shown

1996	1997	1998	1999	2000	2001

Dedication

This book is dedicated to my wife, Marian,
whose encouragement and support has made it possible.
And to my children, Joseph, Francesca,
Andrew, Maria-Carmel, Mario, and Angelina,
for whom I originally wrote this book
and who have been my most important critics.

A special word of thanks is due to Mrs. Louise McGuinn,
the fourth grade teacher of St. Isabella's School, San Rafael,
who has given these lives of the saints the ultimate test
of classroom use over the past few years.

Table of Contents

Introduction

I have been fascinated with the lives of the saints ever since receiving my very first book about our heavenly friends from my parents for my First Holy Communion. I devoured that book, memorizing every word of it, and went looking for more of the same. So began a love affair that has never waned.

This present little volume is simply a writing down of these stories as I have told and retold them to my own children and to the many whom I have had the honor and privilege of catechizing over the years. I have never encountered a child who was not moved — at least somewhat — by the true-life adventures of these heroes and heroines of the Lord. In fact, I have found it most interesting to teach religion to children and youth by using the saints as a "living catechism," drawing from their stories of faith flesh and blood examples of what it means to live and believe as a Catholic Christian.

It was with this catechesis in mind that I have selected the saints included in this book. I have purposely chosen many who are not celebrated in the general liturgical calendar of the Church so that a more varied array of saints and blesseds may be honored. Taken as a whole they offer a colorful mosaic of the Catholic Faith, encompassing such varied backgrounds as apostles, royalty, martyrs and nuns, as well as housewives, single laywomen and teenagers.

This book is meant to be read aloud and should find a welcome home in many Christian families, where it can be used to celebrate feastdays or as bedtime stories. I hope that it will also help to meet the growing demand from catechists and teachers for interesting and informative lives of the saints for children. *Saints for Young Christians* has been used in a local parochial school to assure that its stories are neither too brief so as to be meaningless, nor so lengthy that the student's interest wanes.

Note on the Stages to Sainthood

It may be helpful for the reader to be aware of the stages by which a Catholic reaches that glorious honor of sainthood in the Church.

When a Catholic dies and has a reputation for holiness, the local bishop may initiate the *Cause* or process of canonization of the deceased. Every aspect of the person's life (including letters, conversations, etc.) is examined with great care and detail. What is especially sought after is proof of heroic virtues. Such phenomena as miracles and visions do not help, but actually hinder, the Cause. The findings of this research are passed on to the proper office at the Vatican which oversees the Causes of the Saints. If a favorable decision is given by these officials, the Holy Father confirms their findings and the candidate receives the title of *Venerable*. This is usually the longest step of the process.

To be officially named a *Blessed* of the Church, at least one genuine inexplicable miracle must have been worked by God through the intercession of the Venerable candidate. Once such has been verified, the Pope sets a date for the ceremony of *beatification*. The new Blessed may now receive a feastday and be liturgically honored in a limited way (e.g., by their religious order, in their home diocese, as one's personal patron, etc.)

Finally, at least one additional miracle needs to be granted by God before the Blessed is declared a *Saint* of the universal Church. As with beatification, the Holy Father sets a date for the ceremony of *canonization*. Once canonized, the Saint becomes a model for Christians everywhere and his/her feast may be celebrated by all. The act of canonization, by its nature, is an infallible proclamation by the Church.

It should be noted that the above steps to canonization do not apply to those who die as martyrs. It is the ancient and scriptural belief of Christians that martyrs (those who die for the holy Faith) are brought into Heaven immediately upon death. Thus the Holy Father may (and has, as with St. Maximilian Kolbe) excused the martyr from any or all of the above steps to official sainthood.

The Beautiful Queen of All Saints
Solemnity of the Mother of God — January 1

Do you know who is the greatest of all the saints? Here's a clue: she was chosen by God to become the Mother of His only Son. It is the Blessed Virgin Mary, of course! And she is your mother, too, in the family of God.

Mary (whose name in her Hebrew language was *Miriam*) was

born in Nazareth about 15 years before Jesus' birth. Her parents, Joachim and Ann, had been married a long time before she was born. They were sad because they didn't have any children and offered many prayers to God asking for the gift of a child. One day, Ann had some good news to share with Joachim — they were finally going to have a baby! Nine months later Mary was born, and she was the most beautiful baby they had ever seen. From the very first moment of life in Ann's womb, Mary was filled with God's grace. We call this her *Immaculate Conception*. It made her the holiest of all God's creatures.

As she grew older, Mary grew more beautiful in both body and soul. When she was about 14 years old, she became engaged to be married to Joseph, a strong and handsome carpenter of Nazareth. Before their wedding day something very unusual happened to Mary. The angel Gabriel was sent to her with this message, "God wants you to become the Mother of the long-awaited Savior." What do you think Mary said to the angel? She replied, "I am God's servant. I will do whatever He asks." At that moment the tiny Baby Jesus began to live in Mary's pure womb. We call this visit of the angel to Mary the *Annunciation*. Of course, everyone knows that Jesus was born nine months later in the little town of Bethlehem. Mary never had any other children but Jesus. This is why we call her *Ever Virgin*.

For 30 years Jesus, Mary, and Joseph lived a happy and busy family life in Nazareth. Jesus worked at Joseph's side as a carpenter to help support the family. Mary did all the many things around the house that mothers do to care for their families. Some time after Joseph died, Jesus left home to begin His special work as the Teacher sent to us from God. The Gospels tell us all about His many miracles and teachings. While Jesus did these things, Mary followed Him and listened to all that He said. She became the first and most perfect follower of her Son.

When Our Lord was crucfied on Mt. Calvary, Mary was there beside Him. Even though most of His friends had run away out of fear, she remained faithful to her Son. She stood by His cross and offered her sorrow to God along with the suffering of Jesus. Together, they offered His death to God as a sacrifice to take away our sins. It was on Mt. Calvary that Jesus gave us Mary to be our mother. This happened when He said, "Behold your mother" (*Jn 19:27*). After Jesus rose from the dead and returned to Heaven, Mary stayed with His followers to help them. She prayed with them for the Gift of the Holy Spirit. She told them of the angel's visit and shared her memories about Jesus as a baby and a little child.

When the Twelve Apostles traveled to different lands to preach the Good News about Jesus, Mary went with the Apostle John. They lived in the town of Ephesus in a part of Asia Minor known today as Turkey. After many years it came time for Mary to leave this world and go to live forever with her Son. It all took place during a visit to her relatives in Jerusalem. Mary was so holy and filled with love for God that He did something very special for her. He brought both her body and soul to Heaven. We call this wonderful event Mary's *Assumption* into Heaven.

Mary, the Queen of all Saints, is loved so much by Catholics that we celebrate many feastdays in her honor throughout the year. The most important ones are: Immaculate Conception (Dec. 8), Birth of Mary (Sept. 8), Mother of God (Jan. 1), Annunciation (March 25), and Assumption (Aug. 15). We also honor Mary with many different titles like *Our Blessed Mother, Our Lady, and Mother of God*. Thousands of girls receive a form of her name at Baptism (like Maria, Maura, and Molly) and so do many boys (like Mario and Myles). No other saint has been so loved and honored by Christians for the past 2,000 years.

The Woman Who Saved Paris
St. Genevieve — January 3

Paris, France, is one of the most exciting and beautiful cities of the world. It has long been a center of art, fashion, literature, and romance. But a long time ago, Paris was a sleepy little village which was just starting to become an important town. It was at this time that today's saint lived. Her name was Genevieve, a poor little shepherdess who is now one of the patronesses of France.

Genevieve was born near Paris in the year 424. Her parents were poor but devout Catholics who taught their little girl to love God more than anything else in the world. Genevieve worked as a shepherdess, spending her days in the beautiful hillsides looking after a flock of sheep. When she was seven years old two holy bishops came to her town. One of them noticed how much Genevieve loved God and how she spent so much time in prayer before the Blessed Sacrament. He spoke to her about dedicating her life to God. This was at a time in history before there were such things as religious communities of Sisters. He gave Genevieve a little medal which had a cross on it and told her to wear it always. It was to be a reminder of her dream to one day belong totally to Jesus.

When she was 15, Genevieve was able to make her childhood dream come true. At a religious ceremony the Bishop of Paris blessed her and consecrated her to God. *Consecrated* means giving something or someone to belong to God in a special way. As a sign of her belonging to God the bishop gave her a veil which only consecrated women were allowed to wear. How happy she was to finally belong to God in this special way! Together with some of her friends Genevieve would go throughout the town helping the poor, nursing the sick, and visiting those in prison. God worked many miracles through this holy girl's prayers and she soon became famous all across the land.

At this time in history many towns in France were being invaded by enemy soldiers. These armies attacked Paris and closed off all of its streets. They would not allow anyone to come or go from the city. After a while, the people ran out of food and began to grow hungry. They were just about to surrender their beloved city to the enemy when Genevieve came up with a secret plan. Late one night, while all of Paris was dark and still, she led some of her friends out to the river where they boarded a large raft. Genevieve prayed with all her heart that God would protect them and, sure enough, He did. They floated the raft downstream to the next city where they purchased wheat and other foods. Upon their return to Paris they were cheered by the people! There were shouts of joy, "Hurray for Genevieve! She has saved Paris and us from the enemy!" Many years passed and through them all Genevieve continued to live her life of Christian service and love. She worked some very wonderful miracles: the crippled walked, the blind received sight, and she even raised up a person from the dead!

When Clovis was made the new King of France Genevieve became good friends with the Queen, Clotilda. Together they spoke to the king about becoming a Catholic and were filled with joy when he finally agreed. What a glorious day it was when King Clovis and all of his 3,000 soldiers received the holy Sacrament of Baptism! This was how France became the first all-Catholic country in the world.

As the new year of 512 began, 88-year-old Genevieve became ill. On January 3, she died and all of France was saddened at the news of her death. So many miracles took place that the King and Queen decided to bury Genevieve in the royal church. She has been honored as both a saint and as the protectress of Paris ever since the day she died. French Catholics throughout the world celebrate her feastday every year on January 3.

The Foundress of the First American Sisters

St. Elizabeth Ann Bayley Seton — January 4

T he United States of America is very different from most other countries. We are made up of people from every nation upon the earth, as well as those who are natives of our land. Unlike Europe or Asia we do not have a long history as a nation, nor do we have one main religion. Most U.S. citizens are the descendants

ST. ELIZABETH

ANN SETON

of immigrants, that is, people who have come here from a different land. Today's saint lived at an exciting time when the U.S.A. was just beginning, and she knew many people whom we consider to be famous today. For example, her family was friends with George Washington and they were also related to the Roosevelts, from whom two more of our presidents would come.

Elizabeth Ann Bayley was born in New York City on August 28, 1774. Her father, Dr. Richard Bayley, was an important and rich person in New York. The Bayleys were Protestant Christians called Episcopalians, and Elizabeth's grandfather was a minister in this church. Coming from such a wealthy and well-known family, Elizabeth and her two sisters had everything they could ever want. They especially loved to play the piano, ride horses, and dance.

When she was 19 years old, Elizabeth married William Seton. They loved each other very much and were blessed by God with the gift of five children. The Setons lived in a fancy section of New York City and often gave big parties for their many friends. They were very happy, indeed! But sadness soon came into their lives when William caught a terrible sickness. Hoping that a vacation would be good for his health, the family went to visit some friends who lived in Italy. During the long voyage William's fever grew worse and he died soon after arriving in Europe.

Poor Elizabeth! Her family was in a strange land where they didn't speak the language nor have a home of their own. Her Italian friends were very good Catholics. They welcomed her and the children into their home and helped them in many ways. Most of all, they introduced her to the Catholic Faith. Elizabeth was very attracted by the Real Presence of Jesus in the Eucharist. She especially loved to attend Mass and Benediction.

After returning to the United States, Elizabeth and her children became Catholics, which was a very brave thing to do. A long time ago Catholics were not welcome in the United States. They were picked on and teased because of their beliefs. In some places they were even attacked and their churches were burned to the ground! Many relatives and friends turned away from Elizabeth now that she was a Catholic. They didn't speak to her or invite her to their parties. To have a more peaceful life, the Seton family moved to Baltimore, Maryland, where most American Catholics lived. She opened a little school and soon became a very popular teacher.

At this time there were hardly any priests or Sisters to serve God's people in America. When the Archbishop heard all about Elizabeth's school and of her great love for God, he asked her to start the very first American congregation of Sisters. She agreed and called them the *Sisters of Charity*. As the leader of these Sisters, Elizabeth now became known as Mother Seton. The special works of the Sisters were to teach in schools, care for the sick in hospitals, and look after poor children whose parents had died. With Mother Seton's direction they started the very first parochial schools in our country.

For many years Mother Seton took care of both her five children and her spiritual daughters, the Sisters of Charity. She loved and served the Church with all her heart until her death on January 4, 1821. In 1975 Pope Paul VI declared Mother Seton to be the first American-born saint. Her Sisters of Charity still serve God's people all over America. With them we celebrate the feast of St. Elizabeth Ann Bayley Seton every year on January 4.

The Holy Teacher of Montreal
St. Marguerite Bourgeoys — January 12

Many people talk about the important role that women should have in the work of the Church today. Some think that this is a new idea but the Church and the saints have always known that women are very necessary for spreading the Good News in the world. Think about some of history's most important women.

Without Mary, Jesus would never have been born for us in Bethlehem. Without Queen Isabella of Spain, Columbus would not have set sail to discover the New World. Without Joan of Arc, France would have been conquered by the English. And without today's saint the great land of Canada would not have its beautiful city of Montreal nor its Catholic schools. This important woman was St. Marguerite Bourgeoys, the pioneer teacher of French Canada.

Marguerite was born in France on April 17, 1620. This was at the very same time that the Pilgrims in England were setting sail for the New World upon the Mayflower. Marguerite's father was a candle-maker who owned a little shop in their village. The Bourgeoys had twelve children and enjoyed a happy family life. Little Marguerite loved to play with her many friends and especially liked to dress up in fancy clothes with all kinds of clips and ribbons in her hair. She was a lively girl who was not all that interested in religion and holiness.

When she was 20 years old Marguerite had a change of heart. She stopped thinking so much about fancy clothes and parties, and spent more time in prayer. She also thought about becoming a nun. Then one day she heard stories about the French settlers who had sailed across the ocean to begin new lives in Canada. She felt so sorry for the children there who had no schools where they could learn and have fun like she did as a little girl. She decided to go to Canada herself as a school teacher even though everyone told her it was too dangerous for a single young woman as herself. But Marguerite knew that God wanted her there so she set sail for the New World in 1653. She was 33 years old at the time.

Upon arriving in Canada she settled in Montreal which is now one of Canada's most beautiful and important cities. But back then it was a town struggling to survive and threatened with extinction. There were no schools, no hospitals, and was under constant threat of attack by the fierce Iroquois Indians. Marguerite's work as a school teacher gave the citizens of Montreal hope for the future and the town began to grow. Today she is honored as one of the foundresses of this magnificent city.

In 1676, Marguerite gathered together a group of women to start the *Daughters of the Congregation of Notre Dame*. They were teaching Sisters who opened many schools for the Canadian pioneers and for the local Indian children, too. The special mission of these religious women was to teach others both by word and good example, just as Our Lady had taught the first Christians to be good followers of her Son. Marguerite led these brave Sisters through many dangerous times and places. Their goodness and works helped to make French Canada an important center of the Catholic Faith in the New World.

When Marguerite was 73, she asked another Sister to take over as the leader of the Notre Dame Congregation and spent the rest of her life nursing sick Sisters, visiting schools, and praying for all the people. When an important Sister in the congregation was dying, Marguerite asked God to let her die instead. She felt that the other Sister was needed more than she was. God heard Marguerite's prayer and accepted the gift of her life. She died on January 12, 1700 at 80 years of age. Not very long ago the Pope declared Marguerite Bourgeoys a saint and her feastday is celebrated in Canada on January 12.

The First Monk of Egypt

St. Anthony of the Desert — January 17

C hristians receive from God a special calling to serve Him in the world. This calling is known as a *vocation*. There are four kinds of vocations in life: priesthood, marriage, single life, and religious life. Each one of us has to choose which vocation is best for us. We discover our vocation by prayer and by asking the advice

of people we trust. Today's saint is most famous for being the founder of religious life for Catholic monks of the East.

Anthony was born in Egypt in the year 251. His parents were very wealthy. When they died they left all their treasures to Anthony and his little sister. He was 20 years old at the time. While he was at Mass one day, Anthony heard this Gospel reading: "If you want to become perfect, sell everything that you own and give the money to the poor. Then come and follow me" (Mt 19:21). The Holy Spirit inspired him to obey these words of Jesus. He sold all of his belongings, gave the money to the poor, and began to live a new kind of life.

This new life was totally dedicated to God in a special way. Anthony tried to live like Jesus by not marrying and by living in a simple way. He was obedient to the will of God and did only those things which would please our heavenly Father. He spent his days working in the fields, praying, and reading the Bible. How happy he was to live for God alone! News spread about Anthony's life and soon other men came to join him. They wanted to live like Jesus and become perfect, too!

9

Anthony and his group of friends were called monks. Monks are men who dedicate their lives to God and live in a special house called a monastery. Anthony became the superior or leader of the monks. He gave them a rule, which is a set of instructions on how to live a happy and holy Christian life. He was the first person in history to start the custom of having monks and nuns wear special clothing called habits. This clothing shows others that monks and nuns are specially dedicated to God.

One day the cruel Governor of Egypt began persecuting Christians. Anthony was not afraid of the Governor. He went into the city to help the Christians who were living there. He encouraged them to remain faithful to Jesus and to their holy Catholic Faith. Anthony offered many prayers and acts of penance to God, asking Him to bring an end to this awful persecution. God heard the prayers of His holy servant and soon the persecution ceased.

Towards the end of his life, Anthony became known as a great preacher and miracle-worker. At this time there was a lot of confusion among God's people because of a disobedient priest named Arius. Fr. Arius was teaching people that Jesus wasn't really the Son of God. Anthony was very upset by this false teaching. He reminded everyone that Jesus is truly God the Son, who came down from Heaven and was born of the holy Virgin Mary. He worked many miracles to show the people that his words were true.

In the year 356, when Anthony was 105 years old, he called his monks together and encouraged them to always live holy lives full of love for God and others. Then he bade them farewell and died peacefully. All the people called Anthony a saint and prayed to him for help in their lives. We celebrate the feastday of this holy man of God every year on January 17.

The Girl Who Gave Her Life for Her Mom
Bl. Laura Vicuna — January 22

In the world today there are many couples who live together without being married as husband and wife. They do not follow God's plan that a man and a woman who truly love one another receive His blessing through the Sacrament of Matrimony. It is a sin to live in this way and those who do so are in danger of losing Heaven forever! The girl whom we are honoring today knew how important it is for couples to live according to God's plan. She bravely gave up her life for her own mother who was living with a man to whom she was not married. This girl's name is Blessed Laura Vicuna.

BLESSED LAURA

◆ VICUÑA ◆

Laura was born in the South American country of Chile on April 5, 1891. Her father was a soldier who was killed in battle when she was only 3 years old. In order to find a better life for Laura and her little sister, Julia, Mrs. Vicuna took them to live on a farm where she found work as a cook. It was here that she met the man who was to be nothing but trouble in her life. His name was Manuel Mora. Mr. Mora was a rich and powerful person who owned much of the land in town. He selfishly offered to take care of Mrs. Vicuna and her daughters as long as the poor widow would consent to live with him without getting married. Unfortunately, Mrs. Vicuna agreed to this plan.

When Laura was 8 years old she and Julia were sent to a boarding school run by the Salesian Sisters of St. John Bosco. Here Laura learned all about God and of His great love for

11

us. She quickly became one of the most popular girls in school because of her kindness and friendliness towards all. Laura began to spend more time in prayer and received the sacraments as often as possible. She decided to become a Salesian Sister when she grew up, but this was never to be.

During the summer of 1901, 10-year-old Laura began to understand what kind of life her mother was living. While on vacation from school she noticed that Mr. Mora gave her and Julia a lot of attention in ways that made her feel uncomfortable. For two years Laura offered many prayers, and even the gift of her life, to God that her mother would move out of this evil man's house. Finally, on January 14, 1904, her prayers were answered.

On that night Mrs. Vicuna took her belongings and her two daughters to another home. This made Mr. Mora furious and he knew it was all because of Laura. After having gotten drunk, he showed up at their new home and demanded that they return to his farm. Laura told him to go away and then walked out of the house. Suddenly, she heard her mother scream! Turning around, Laura saw Mr. Mora coming towards her. She ran with all her might to the Salesian Sisters, but she never made it to their door. Mr. Mora grabbed her and threw the brave girl to the ground. He beat and whipped her and then left her for dead. Poor Laura! She suffered from this beating for several days and said to her Mom, "I am happy to offer my life for you. I have asked Our Lord for this." Mrs. Vicuna now understood how awful her life had been and she promised Laura that she would change her ways.

On January 22, 1904, Laura Vicuna died as a result of the beating she had received. She was just 13 years old. That very same night Mrs. Vicuna kept the promise she made to her daughter and received the Sacrament of Reconciliation. Laura's unselfish gift of her own life had helped to save her mother's soul. Pope John Paul II declared Laura a Blessed of the Church in 1989 and the Salesian Order celebrates her feastday every year on January 22.

The Teacher Who Was Loved by Everyone

St. Angela Merici — January 27

A long time ago people thought that only boys needed to go to school. They believed that learning to read and write were things which only men needed to know. Today's saint didn't believe that this was true. She dedicated her whole life to the education of girls because she knew that women are very important in the world. Her name is Angela Merici and she was a very great woman herself.

Angela was born on March 21, 1474, in the northern Italian town of Desenzano. When she was growing up many new and interesting events were happening in the world, especially the discoveries of so many new lands. Her parents were very good Catholics and they made sure that the Merici children learned all about God, the Blessed Virgin, and the Catholic Faith. One night, after Mrs. Merici had read the children a bedtime story about the saints, little 5-year-old Angela said, "Mommy, I want to become a saint, too!"

When she was 15, Angela's parents and sister died. So she and her brother went to live with their uncle. He was very rich and had a beautiful home. He wanted Angela to get married but she had already decided to give herself to God alone. One day, while Angela was saying her prayers in the parish church, God spoke to her and told her what she was to do with her life. He said, "Go to the town of Brescia. There you will start a community of women whose members will teach young girls and serve the poor."

13

Angela, who always tried to do what God wanted of her, moved to the town of Brescia. She gathered together 12 friends and started the new community. They did not become Sisters but remained lay-women who were totally dedicated to God. Angela and her companions made special promises to God called *vows*. They promised to live as Jesus and Mary had lived: in poverty, purity, and obedience. The name of the new group was the *Company of St. Ursula*, or just *Ursulines* for short. St. Ursula was a young woman who had dedicated herself to God. She was a good model for Angela and her companions. The Ursulines lived in their own homes but met together every day to pray with one another. They carried out many good works, such as teaching poor girls, nursing the sick, and caring for the needy.

Angela and her friends were loved very much by the people they served and their schools for girls became very popular. More and more ladies joined the community and soon the Company of St. Ursula spread out to many different towns and countries. When Angela was 66 years old her health became very poor and her body grew weaker. On January 27, 1540, Angela died surrounded by her companions and friends. Many people began praying to her right away because they believed she was truly in Heaven. Soon afterwards the Pope declared Angela Merici to be a saint.

Angela's companions continued to serve God and His people throughout the world. They divided into two kinds of Ursuline groups. One group became Sisters and they were the very first nuns to start convents in America. The other group remained laywomen just like Angela had been, and they have over 5,000 members today. We celebrate the feastday of this holy foundress and teacher every year on January 27.

The Brave Girl of Sicily
St. Agatha — February 5

Throughout the history of the world there have been rulers who claimed to be like gods. The ancient Roman Emperors used to think that they were gods. They made the people worship them and most of citizens did whatever their leaders wanted. But the Christians could not do this. They knew that there is but one

God and that the only Person Who is both God and Man is Jesus. They refused to worship the Emperors because it was against the First Commandment which says, "I alone am the Lord your God; you shall worship no other gods besides Me." This made the Emperors furious! They ordered their soldiers to arrest the Christians and to kill those who would not give up their faith in Christ. Today's saint was one of these early Christian martyrs. As you probably know, a martyr is someone who is killed because of their faith in God. Those who die as martyrs go straight to Heaven!

Agatha was born around the year 253 in the town of Catania on the Italian island of Sicily. When Agatha was a teenager a young pagan man named Quintian fell in love with her. But Agatha had already fallen in love with Someone else: Jesus our Savior. As a sign of her pure love for Christ she promised God that she would never marry. When Quintian heard of this, he became very upset. He was friends with the Emperor and so he decided to tell him that Agatha was a Christian. He wanted to have her arrested so that he could "get even" with her.

15

The soldiers arrested Agatha and put her into a house with some evil women who did not know or love God. They did all kinds of sinful things and used very bad language. In this way, the Emperor thought that he could make Agatha give up her pure love for Jesus. But he did not know how strong she was in spirit. She prayed to God saying, "O Lord Jesus Christ, You know that I love You with all my heart. I want to belong to You alone. Help me to overcome these temptations of the devil."

When Quintian learned that Agatha still refused to give up her faith, he told the soldiers to torture her. They hit and whipped her, but she still would not give up her love for God. After giving Agatha a horrible beating the soldiers locked her up in a dark prison. Late that night, the Apostle St. Peter appeared to the brave girl in a vision and miraculously healed all her wounds. He said that her sufferings would shortly be over and that she would soon come to live forever in Heaven.

Four days later, Quintian commanded the soldiers to kill Agatha. Before they carried out this order, the brave girl of Sicily prayed to God with these words, "O Lord, my Creator, give me patience to suffer for You. Receive my soul into Heaven." Upon finishing her prayer, the soldiers cut off her head, and thus Agatha died as a martyr for Jesus.

The Christians of Sicily almost immediately honored her as a saint and prayed to her for help in all their needs. As a special remembrance (called a relic) they saved Agatha's veil. It would prove to be a powerful sign of her protection and love for the people. The town of Catania is located near a great volcano called Mt. Etna. Many years after Agatha's martyrdom, the volcano began to shoot out steam and threatened to erupt. The Christians remembered Agatha and took her veil in a procession of prayer around the city. Suddenly, Mt. Etna became quiet and still! The people cheered their saint and to this day her veil is still honored as a special relic. St. Agatha became one of the most popular girl saints in the Church and she is mentioned by name at Mass in Eucharistic Prayer I. Her yearly feastday is February 5.

The First Teaching Brother of Ecuador
Bl. Miguel Muñoz — February 9

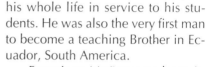

T eaching is one of the most important jobs in the whole world. Can you imagine not knowing how to read? Or how to write? Or how to do addition? Teachers are also very special people. Everyone has a favorite teacher who helped them in one way or another. Today's saint was one of these dedicated teachers who spent his whole life in service to his students. He was also the very first man to become a teaching Brother in Ecuador, South America.

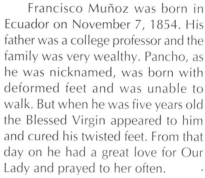

Francisco Muñoz was born in Ecuador on November 7, 1854. His father was a college professor and the family was very wealthy. Pancho, as he was nicknamed, was born with deformed feet and was unable to walk. But when he was five years old the Blessed Virgin appeared to him and cured his twisted feet. From that day on he had a great love for Our Lady and prayed to her often.

When he was nine years of age Pancho enrolled in a new school run by the Christian Brothers. These men were specially dedicated to God and to the education of boys. Pancho used to spend all of his free time at school and was very attracted to the Brothers' way of life. As a young teenager he decided to become a Christian Brother, too. His parents were very upset when they learned about this decision! They didn't mind his dedicating his life to God, but they thought that such a rich and intelligent boy should become a priest. After many months of prayer and discussion they finally gave Pancho the permission he needed to enter religious life.

17

In 1868, 14-year-old Pancho officially joined the Christian Brothers and received the new religious name of Brother Miguel. His superiors knew that he was very smart so they were not surprised when Brother Miguel wrote his first textbook at the age of 17. It was the first of many books, poems, and songs that he would write. Miguel became a very popular teacher and his students all agreed that he was most kind and gentle in class. Brother never got angry or impatient with anyone.

Being a good teacher, however, was not what made Brother Miguel holy. *Holiness* means doing everything for the love of God and for the good of others. This was the secret to his saintly way of life. He once wrote these words about holiness in his journal, "I will give myself completely to Jesus so that He can use me exactly as He wishes. I want everything I do, every word I write, every book I read to give glory to God."

When he was 45 years old, Brother Miguel was sent to Europe to translate books into Spanish. He missed Ecuador very much but was glad to go where he was needed. While living in Spain Brother caught a bad cold. In those days doctors didn't have all the wonderful medicines which we know about today, so Brother's cold grew worse and soon began to hurt his lungs. On February 9, 1910, Brother Miguel Muñoz died far away from his family and homeland. Many miracles began to happen to those who asked his prayers, and in 1977 the Pope declared him to be a Blessed of the Church. The Christian Brothers celebrate his feast every year on February 9.

The Saint of Love and Friendship
St. Valentine — February 14

Every year on St. Valentine's Day friends send special messages of love and affection to one another. But few people know the real meaning of the words, "Be my Valentine." This traditional greeting honors a real-life saint who lived almost 2,000 years ago.

Valentine was a holy priest who lived in the ancient city of Rome. He was greatly loved by the Christians whom he served with all his heart. During one of the many Roman persecutions of the Church, Valentine was arrested and thrown into prison. The Emperor made all kinds of wonderful promises of riches and pleasures to Valentine, trying to get him to deny his faith in Jesus. But the brave priest would not betray Our Lord. So on February 14, about the year 270 A.D., Valentine was beaten with clubs and then beheaded. In this way he had the honor of proving his love for Christ by dying as a martyr.

According to some ancient Christian stories, Valentine used to secretly send little notes of love and encouragement to his Christian friends while he was in prison. Many people believe that this is why we send *Valentines* on his feastday. Other people think that the Valentine custom is celebrated on February 14 because that was the day of the year when pagan Romans used to choose their boyfriends and girlfriends. When these pagans converted to Christianity they kept up this custom but carried it out in honor of St. Valentine.

Whatever the reason for our Valentines custom, the important thing to remember on this day is *love*. The Bible tells us that "God is love, and those who live in love live in God, and God lives in them" (*1 Jn 4:16*). True love means that we love God more than anyone else and that we love our neighbors as ourselves. It means that we try to be kind, patient, and generous to others, never being rude or mean to them. This is the way that we should truly celebrate February 14 as the feast of St. Valentine, the patron of true Christian love and friendship.

The Seven Holy Servants of Mary

Founders of the Servite Order — February 17

SEVEN HOLY

AVE MARIA

◆ FOUNDERS ◆

lorence, Italy is one of the most beautiful cities of Europe. It has been a center of magnificent art and great learning for centuries. Florence was also the home of some of the most wealthy people of Italy. Today's saints lived in this city almost eight hundred years ago. God chose them to start a new religious order in the Church which has thousands of members in every part of the world today.

In the year 1225, seven young businessmen of Florence met together to form a kind of prayer group in honor of Mary, the Mother of Jesus. They all came from wealthy families and made lots of money as merchants. But they were more interested in serving God than in storing up great treasures. Their names were Buonfiglio, Alexis, Benedict, Bartholomew, Ricovero, Gerard and John. The seven friends used to meet everyday for prayer. They asked the Blessed Virgin to show them what they were to do with their lives.

On the feast of Mary's Assumption into Heaven, August 15, 1225, Our Lady answered their prayers by appearing to them in a vision. She told then to leave the noise and activity of the city. Mary wanted them to live a life of prayer and penance in the quiet hills nearby. After receiving their bishop's blessing the young men built a little chapel and monastery in the mountains. They spent their days in silence, prayer, and self-denial.

Soon afterwards, the people of Florence began to come to them in great numbers to ask for prayers and advice. They begged the monks to come back to the city to serve the people who lived there. The seven companions turned to prayer to learn what God wanted them to do.

On April 13, 1240, the Mother of God again appeared to the group and showed them a black *habit* or robe that was to become their special uniform. She also gave them a name for their community, the *Servants of Mary*. The seven friends felt that this was a sign for them to return to the city and so they did. This was the beginning of the *Servite Order*. The new order grew very quickly and it soon had hundreds of priests and Brothers. Many women also asked to become Servants of Mary Sisters and laypeople joined the community as Secular Servites. The work of all of these members was to preach the Good News about Jesus, to care for the needy, and to spread devotion to the holy Mother of God.

Over the years the seven holy founders of the Order left this world for Heaven one by one. The last to die was Brother Alexis who also became the most famous of them all. He lived to be 110 years old. It was his niece, St. Juliana, who started the first Servite nuns. These businessmen who gave up their riches to serve God and others were declared saints by the Holy Father and are good models for us today. They remind us of Jesus' words, "You cannot serve both God and money" (*Mt 6:24*). The feast of the Seven Holy Founders of the Servite Order is celebrated every year on February 17.

The Woman Who Gave Her Life for Priests
St. Anne Line — February 26

About 400 years ago, King Henry VIII of England decided to make himself the Head or Leader of the Catholics in his land. Of course, this was not really possible because Jesus made the Pope the Leader of all Catholics no matter where they live. When the Holy Father reminded King Henry of this truth, the King became

ST. ANNE

LINE

very angry and started his own new church. He called it the Church of England and its members became known as Episcopalians. In order to get English Catholics to join his new church, the King declared laws which made it a crime to be a Catholic in England! Many brave Catholics ignored these new laws and a lot of them became martyrs. One of these was the saint whom we will learn about today. Her name was Anne Line.

Anne Heighman was born into an Episcopalian family in England but when she was a teenager she converted to the Catholic Faith. This upset her parents so much that they told her to leave home! As she sadly packed her things, Anne remembered these words of Jesus, "If you do not love Me more than your family, you cannot be My follower" (cf. *Lk 14:26-27*). She prayed a lot for her family that they, too, would find joy in the Catholic Faith.

At 19 years of age, Anne met and married Roger Line, who was also a convert to the Faith. They had a wonderful marriage and loved each other very much. Together, they did all they could to help English Catholics remain faithful to Jesus. One of the most special but dangerous things they did was to hide priests in their home. You see, the laws made it illegal to be a priest or to attend Mass in England. To hide a priest or to allow Mass to be celebrated in your home was a crime punishable by death! But the Lines didn't care about these unjust laws. They continued to take care of priests and to have Masses offered in their home.

One day when Roger was at a secret Mass, the police raided the house and took him prisoner. When they brought him to court, the judge decided to punish him by banishing him from England. This meant that he would be sent out of the country and could never return to his homeland. Sadly, he was shipped to France and he never saw his dear wife again. Instead of frightening her, Roger's arrest and punishment only made Anne more dedicated to the special work of caring for priests.

Anne contacted the Jesuit Fathers to offer them her help. She was put in charge of a house where the priests could hide from the police and where they could secretly celebrate Mass. Even when she became very ill, Anne kept up this good and dangerous work. To protect her from the police, the priests gave her the secret code name of "Mrs. Martha." They called her this in honor of St. Martha who used to take good care of Jesus and His Twelve Apostles.

On February 2, 1601, Anne was helping a priest get ready to celebrate Mass for the feast of the Presentation of Jesus in the Temple. Suddenly, the police broke open the doors of the house! They arrested Anne and put her in prison. In court the judge sentenced her to death. She bravely said to him, "Sir, I am not afraid to die and go to Heaven. I only wish that I could have taken care of thousands of more priests." What a heroic and courageous woman she was!

A few days later the police carried out the death sentence. Before dying, Anne forgave her killers and prayed that all of England would become Catholic once again. Many years later the Pope declared Anne Line and many other English martyrs to be saints of the Church. English Catholics celebrate the holiness and bravery of St. Anne Line every year on her feastday of February 26.

The Servant of Suffering Americans
Bl. Katharine Drexel — March 3

Not very long ago the western United States was a land of wild horses and roaming buffalo. For thousands of years it was the home of the Indians who are also called *Native Americans.* When the pioneers settled our land they were often very mean to the Indians. They would steal their land and claim it as their own.

BL. KATHERINE

DREXEL

Many Americans were also very cruel to the African-Americans who had been brought to our land as slaves. People made fun of them and would not treat them with dignity or respect. God did not abandon these suffering Americans. He chose a brave woman to become their servant and friend. She would stand up for them and help them to walk proudly as children of God and citizens of the United States.

Katharine Drexel was born on November 26, 1858 in the historic city of Philadelphia, Pennsylvania. Her family was very wealthy and famous. Even today, the Drexel name is well known in the world of business. The Drexels were also very good Catholics. They loved their faith as the most important of all their treasures, and they gave large sums of money to the Church for the care of the poor and needy.

As a little girl Kate (as she was called) loved to play with her dolls, have make believe tea parties, and pass time in the company of her two sisters. As they grew older all three girls developed a deep love for the poor, but it was Kate who would give them more than just money. She would give the gift of her life. One day two visiting priests told her all about the suffering of the African and Native Americans. Their stories touched her generous heart and, after much prayer and advice from her bishop, Kate started a new religious community called the *Sisters of the Blessed Sacrament.* Their special work was to devote themselves completely to the service of these suffering and neglected Americans.

Now known as Mother Drexel, she welcomed many young women into her new sisterhood. They opened schools, hospitals, orphanages, and missions throughout the United States. These courageous Sisters of the Blessed Sacrament began the first university for African-Americans in Louisiana, and became voices for civil rights when this was a very dangerous thing to do. Filled with the spirit of Christian love and service, they carried out many works of mercy on the various Indian reservations across the land.

Mother Drexel became well-known and loved in the United States and abroad. For 64 years she led the Blessed Sacrament Sisters and spoke up for the needs of these suffering Americans. Finally, on March 3, 1955, this generous mother of the neglected died at the age of 96. In 1988, Katharine Drexel was declared a Blessed of the Church by Pope John Paul II. Inspired by her example, the Sisters she founded continue to speak out and work for racial justice in service to the African and Native American peoples. The feast of Blessed Katharine Drexel is celebrated in the U.S.A. on March 3.

The Brother and Servant of the Sick
St. John of God — March 8

ST. JOHN

OF GOD

The saint we are going to learn about today had a most unusual life. He left home as a child, grew up in a foster family, and then lived a sinful life as a soldier. Most people would give such a person little hope of becoming a saint. But God's grace can work great changes in our lives! This man became one of the most generous and loving of Christ's saints.

John was born in Portugal on March 8, 1495, just three years after the discovery of America. As a little boy he heard all the exciting stories about explorers such as Columbus. When he was eight years old, John disappeared from home never to return. It is not known if he ran away or was kidnapped. Three years later John found himself in the land of Spain where he was adopted by a foster family. They treated him just like their own son and raised him to be a good Catholic boy. Over the years John grew older and taller, becoming very handsome and strong.

When he was 28 years old, John joined the army in search of a more exciting life. The other soldiers did not always live good lives. They got drunk, gambled their money away, and did other sinful things. At first John tried to remain a good Christian but he soon followed their bad example. He wanted to be accepted by the soldiers and to become "one of the crowd."

One day, when the soldiers were out on a mission, John was thrown from his horse. While waiting for help to arrive, he thought about how bad a life he was living. He decided to give up his sinful ways and return to the practice of the Catholic Faith. He was about 38 years old at the time. The first thing he did was to make a good confession to the parish priest. Then he left the army and set up a little shop where he sold religious articles and good books. John liked his new business but he felt that God wanted him to do some other kind of work. He wanted to serve the poor in some way.

John went to the town of Granada, Spain, where he began taking care of the sick. At that time in history hospitals were very horrible places. The nurses often ignored their patients and some were very mean to them. Because of this many sick people refused to go to doctors or to the hospital. To help them, John opened his own hospital where everyone was treated with love and gentleness. He would walk the streets of Granada looking for sick people. If he found some who could not walk he would pick them up and carry them across town to his hospital. As a sign of his blessing upon John's work, the Archbishop named him *Brother John of God* and gave him a special robe to wear as a symbol of his dedication to the Lord.

Brother John was a person of much prayer. He went to Mass daily and received Holy Communion every morning. He had a special love for our Blessed Mother Mary, and also for St. Raphael the Archangel, whom the Bible tells us is the Angel of Healing. Brother John of God grew very holy. He tried to do everything out of love for God and for others. Soon other men came to help him in his work of Christian service to the sick. They prayed and worked together for the good of God's people.

Worn out by his many years of unselfish dedication, Brother John developed serious heart problems and had to enter his own hospital as a patient. On his 55th birthday — March 8, 1550 — his nurses found him kneeling in front of the crucifix. He was dead. When news of his death spread throughout the city, people began praying to him right away. They were sure he had gone straight to Heaven. The Holy Father declared Brother John of God a saint and made him the patron of the sick and the dying, of nurses, and of hospitals.

His helpers organized themselves into a new religious community called the *Hospitaller Brothers of St. John of God.* Today these dedicated men can be found all over the world, serving God and the sick as doctors, nurses, medical technicians, and in many other ways. One of their special tasks is to serve as the personal doctors and nurses to the Pope. With them we celebrate the yearly feastday of St. John of God on March 8.

Mother to the Poor and Needy

St. Frances of Rome — March 9

The life of St. Francesca (Frances) of Rome was never dull or boring. God called her to serve Him in every way possible for a 14th century woman: rich and then poor, wife and mother, then widow and nun. And all this within the short span of 56 years! Born in 1384 to a rich and noble Roman family, Frances was married at age 13 to Lorenzo Panziano, one of Rome's wealthiest young men. Blessed with three children, they enjoyed 40 years of marriage during which, it was said, they never spoke an unkind word to one another!

Frances devoted herself wholeheartedly to her life as a wife and mother. Though she loved to spend time in prayer before the Blessed Sacrament, her household affairs often made it impossible for her to get to church. When asked if this bothered her, Frances replied, "A mother must often leave God at the altar in order to find Him present in duties of the home."

Realizing that God gave her family great wealth in order to help the poor, Frances donated large sums of money to many charitable works. But she went even further and gave the gift of herself. She personally cared for the sick, comforted the dying, fed the hungry, and protected the weak from their rich landlords. Her love for God's poor was so great that once she even sold all of her jewelry and best dresses in order to provide money for them! On another occasion, her prayers to God brought a poor widow's dead infant back to life!

In the midst of all this goodness, many of Frances' friends began to gossip about her saying, "Imagine a Lady of Rome entering the filthy shacks of the poor and actually touching those who live there!" Frances soon found that many of her relatives and friends were turning away from her. Yet she knew she was doing the right thing. She was following the Gospel teachings of Jesus. She continued her works of mercy while praying for those who persecuted her.

At this same time other sufferings entered her life. Her husband and a son were taken as prisoners of war, family fortunes dwindled to almost nothing, and her two other children died from severe illnesses. Did these things shake Frances' faith in the love of God? Never. She bravely accepted these events and carried on with her family life and religious activities. She gave even more to God by starting a new community of Sisters called *Benedictine Oblates*. These dedicated women carried out many good works for the poor and needy.

At this time of deep suffering, God gave Frances the very special gift of the visible companionship of her Guardian Angel. They would pray and talk about God together. The angel protected Frances when she made her oftentimes dangerous errands to the homes of the poor. This gift reminds us of our own guardian angels who are special friends sent by God to help us live good Christian lives. By their prayers they help us reach Heaven our true home.

In 1436, Lorenzo died and Frances became a Benedictine Oblate, spending the last four years of her life as superior of the convent. The people came to her in great numbers everyday asking her help in their many needs. When she died, on March 9, 1440, the poor felt that they had lost a most loving mother. The world-wide Church celebrates St. Frances every year on her feastday of March 9, and has chosen her as the heavenly patroness of wives and mothers.

The Bishop Who Made Ireland Catholic
St. Patrick — March 17

Every year on March 17 everyone seems to think that they are Irish! The color green shines out from everywhere, and all kinds of people celebrate the day from sunrise to sunset. It has become such a popular holiday that, in the midst of all the fun and parties, we often forget *who* we are celebrating and *why*. The

who is a very great saint, Patrick of Ireland, and the *why* is because through his works millions of people have become Catholic Christians!

St. Patrick was born of Roman parents in the year 385, in Scotland, so he wasn't even Irish himself! We know very little about his childhood. In the story of his life, Patrick tells us that when he was 14 years old he was kidnapped by pirates. They took him as a slave to Ireland where he lived for the next six years as a shepherd. At this time in history Ireland was a *pagan* land where the people did not know about God our Father or the Lord Jesus Christ. They belonged to the Druid religion which had some horrible practices including that of human sacrifice! Patrick prayed for protection and for help in getting back home to his parents. When he was 20 years old, he was able to escape and returned to his family in Scotland. How happy they were to see their boy alive and well after all those years!

A few years later, Patrick decided to become a priest. When the Pope asked for missionaries to send to Ireland he volunteered for this mission. Imagine freely going back to the very same people who had made him a slave! But Patrick was full of love for the Irish people and wanted to tell them all about Jesus and His Good News of salvation. After the Pope made him a bishop, Patrick set sail for the *Emerald Isle* with a small group of missionary priests.

Upon arrival in Ireland, Patrick headed straight for the castle of the chief king. He knew that if the king would become a Catholic, then all of the people would ask for baptism as well. As he was on the way to the palace, Patrick thought of the many three leaf clovers (called shamrocks) which grew all over the land. They reminded him of God, the *Blessed Trinity*, Father, Son, and Holy Spirit. Just as the shamrock is but one plant with three leaves, so is there only one God but three Persons in the one God. This is why we use shamrocks as decorations on his feastday. God blessed Patrick's meeting with the king. He received permission to go throughout the whole land telling everyone the Good News about Jesus.

By the time Bishop Patrick died on March 17, 461, after 30 years of missionary work, almost every person in Ireland had become a Catholic Christian! But this isn't the end of the story. The Irish Catholics loved their new Faith so much that many of them became missionaries, too, just like St. Patrick. They went to other lands to spread the Good News of Jesus' life, death, and Resurrection. Many centuries later our own nation received thousands of these Irish priests, Brothers, and Sisters.

St. Patrick is a saint who is "catchy." This means that once you learn about him you love him and want to become like him. You, too, can become a "St. Patrick" by telling at least one other person the Good News about Jesus and His Catholic Church. What a great way to really celebrate March 17 as the feastday of St. Patrick!

The Man Who Was Closest to Jesus
St. Joseph — March 19 and May 1

To be the father of a family is a very special but difficult life. Dads don't get to spend a lot of time with their families, but this doesn't mean that they don't love them! They show their love in many ways and one important way is by going to work to earn money for such things as food, shelter and clothing. Dads make many sacrifices so that their wives and children can be happy and have all that they need. This has been true about fathers ever since God created the first man and woman.

ST. JOSEPH

OF NAZARETH

About 2,000 years ago there lived the greatest father in the whole world. He was a good and loving man, very holy and always thinking about others. He lived with the best wife any man ever married and his adopted Son was the Savior of the world. Do you know his name? It was Joseph of Nazareth.

Joseph was born about 20 years before Jesus' birth. He was a member of the ancient royal family of King David. Over the centuries the royal family lost its rule over the kingdom and by the time Joseph was born they were poor. As a little boy Joseph went to school at the Jewish synagogue (church) where he learned to write and to read the Scriptures.

When he grew older Joseph decided to become a carpenter and opened up a little shop in Nazareth. He spent his days making beautiful furniture and other objects. As a young man he was encouraged to find a wife. At that time another family of Nazareth was looking for a good husband for their daughter,

Mary. And so it happened that Joseph the Carpenter and Mary, the daughter of Joachim and Ann, became engaged.

Then one day, soon after their engagement, Mary came to Joseph's shop to share a special secret with him. She told him how an angel had appeared to her with a message from God. She had been chosen to become the Mother of the Messiah or Savior of God's people! Joseph knew that Mary would never lie but he had a hard time accepting her story. He asked God to show him the truth. The Lord gave Joseph a dream in which the same angel came to him and assured him that Mary's story was true. He was to adopt and love the Savior as his very own son and give Him the name, Jesus.

Everyone knows what happened after this. Joseph and Mary had to travel to the little town of Bethlehem and, while they were there, she gave birth to her baby boy. Angels announced His birth to poor shepherds, and wise men from the East followed a miraculous star to find the Newborn King. After a few years, the Holy Family of Jesus, Mary, and Joseph returned to live in their hometown of Nazareth. Jesus went to school, Joseph kept up his work in the carpentry shop, and Mary did all the many things that mothers do to serve their families. As Our Lord grew older He, too, became a carpenter and worked side-by-side with His adopted father.

Before Jesus was 30 years old Joseph fell ill and died. How blessed he was to have lived so long in the loving company of Our Lord and Our Lady! Because of this Christians have honored St. Joseph as the second greatest saint in Heaven. The greatest, of course, is our Blessed Mother. Since Jesus and Mary were with him at death, we also honor St. Joseph as the patron or helper of the dying. He is also the patron of many people and places: husbands, fathers, workers, religious Brothers, and several nations all claim him as their special saint. Since he is so important to Christians, every Wednesday of the week is dedicated to him and he has two feastdays as well. On March 19 we celebrate his vocation as the husband of Mary and foster father of Jesus. On May 1 we honor him as "the Worker."

The Layman Who Became an Archbishop

St. Turibius of Mongrovejo — March 23

ST. TORIBIO

He has sent me to proclaim Good News to the poor..

DE MONGROVEJO

After the Spanish explorers had discovered South America many *conquistadors* or conquerors came with great armies to take over the land and the native people. These rich and powerful men often did many horrible things. They killed many of the Indians and made others their slaves. The Church hoped to help these poor people by sending missionaries to the New World. They brought the Good News of salvation to these people and worked for social justice. *Social justice* means that all people are treated fairly no matter if they are rich or poor. Today's saint was one of these good and loving missionaries. His name is St. Turibius of Mongrovejo.

Turibius (in the Spanish language, the name is spelled Toribio) was born in Spain in 1538. He was from a very wealthy family and grew up to become a brilliant university professor of law. He was so wise that the King of Spain appointed him a judge. Before long, Turibius was well-known throughout the land of Spain.

What is most unusual in his life is that the Pope made him the Archbishop of Lima, Peru, even though he wasn't even a priest! Turibius wrote letters to both the Pope and the King reminding them that he was only a layman. But they wouldn't change their minds. So Turibius accepted this mission and received the Sacrament of Holy Orders in the year 1581. A few days later the 43-year-old Archbishop set sail for South America.

The first thing Archbishop Turibius did after arriving in Peru was

35

to visit every village, church, and mission in his archdiocese. This took seven years and included many dangerous journeys though jungles filled with wild animals. The holy Archbishop was saddened at what he saw on these visits. The rich Spanish people lived in fancy homes with lots of servants, while the poor natives were often homeless and hungry. Turibius decided that many changes needed to be made in Peru. He wrote to the King of Spain begging him to stop the horrible treatment of the Indians.

Archbishop Turibius opened schools where the poor could learn skills to support their families. He had Bibles and catechisms printed in the Indian languages so that they could also learn about God and of His great love for them. Turibius spent most of his time traveling to the many parishes throughout the land preaching the holy Word of God and celebrating the sacraments. It was he who gave the Sacrament of Confirmation to two other saints of Peru, Rose of Lima and Martin de Porres. After twenty-five years as Archbishop of Lima, Turibius's unselfish life came to an end while he was on one of his many visits to the poor. He was canonized a saint many years later and has become a good model for the many missionaries today who spread the Gospel and work for social justice in Latin America. His feastday is celebrated on March 23.

The Doctor Who Loved Everyone
St. Joseph Moscati — March 29

St. Joseph

"I was sick and you took care of me."

Gospel of St Matthew

Moscati, M.D.

Sometimes we think that the saints were not ordinary people like us. Perhaps it's because so many of them lived hundreds of years ago, or died as martyrs for Jesus, or were great miracle-workers. Today's saint was very much like us and he lived not very long ago. His life reminds us that *everyone* is called to holiness and that we can serve God by doing our daily work for the good of others.

Joseph Moscati was born in Italy in the year 1881. That's around the time that many of our great grandparents were born. Joe was a fun-loving boy who did well at school and liked to play sports. His family was very rich and they used to give lots of money, food, and clothing to the poor. The Moscatis believed that God gave some families more money than others so that they could have the honor of taking care of the poor. They taught Joe that God has a very special love for the poor and for those who dedicate their lives to serving the poor. This made him think very much about what he was going to be when he grew up.

When Joe was a teenager, he decided to become a doctor just like his dad. He felt that as a doctor he could serve the sick and the poor in a special way. Joe studied very hard and became one of the most famous doctors in Italy. He was put in charge of a large hospital where he cared for the sick and dying. The young doctor also worked as a professor of a medical school, training others in the practice of medicine.

Everyone noticed that Dr. Joe

Moscati was somehow different from most other physicians. There was something about him that made people think about Jesus, and of how our Lord used to cure the sick and heal their wounds. The "secret" to this special feeling people had about him came from his deep love for God. He used to start every morning by attending Mass and receiving the Body of Christ in Holy Communion. He loved our Blessed Mother very much and prayed the rosary everyday. Becoming holy was more important to Dr. Joe than anything else. He knew that the holier he became, the better doctor he would be. As a special gift to God, Dr. Joe decided not to get married and have a family of his own. Instead, he chose to remain single in order to devote himself more fully to the service of the sick and the poor.

When young Joe first became "Dr. Moscati" he began the practice of serving the poor free of charge. He would even go to their homes at any time of the day or night, something which some doctors did only for their rich and famous patients. Even today some of these people, who were little kids when Dr. Joe cared for them, remember his home visits and say he was a loving, warm and joyful person.

As a Catholic physician, Dr. Joe Moscati tried to serve the *whole person*, believing that people need to have both a healthy body and a healthy soul. While he cared for sick bodies, Dr. Joe always called on priests to heal souls, especially through the Sacrament of Reconciliation. Sometimes, Dr. Moscati's patients would actually be cured in body only after they had "cured" their souls of sin in confession. God gave Dr. Joe a special gift of knowing in his heart when patients needed the Sacrament of Reconciliation to cure their sicknesses.

Dr. Joe died suddenly one evening in 1927, at the young age of 46. How he was missed by all his patients! But they truly believed that God had taken him to Heaven, and so they began to pray to him for help in their illnesses. So many people were cured by Dr. Joe's prayers that in 1987, our Holy Father, Pope John Paul II, declared him an official saint of the Catholic Church. The yearly feastday of Joseph Moscati, MD is March 29.

The Sinful Woman Who Became a Great Saint

St. Mary of Egypt — April 2

One of the most amazing things about the saints is that some of them started out as great sinners. As you know, sin is disobedience against the holy law of God. It means that we choose to love ourselves more than God or our neighbor. All sin is horrible but mortal sin is the worst of all. *Mortal sin* means that we

SAINT MARY

Turn away from sin and believe in Jesus

OF EGYPT

freely do something which is seriously wrong and that we no longer have God's life within us. Those who commit mortal sin and are not sorry for having done so cannot enter the Kingdom of Heaven. Today's saint was a great sinner who lived a life of mortal sin for many years. But she turned to God for forgiveness and has become one of the greatest saints of the Church. Her name is St. Mary of Egypt.

Mary was born in Egypt in the year 354. We do not know much about her childhood but we do know that as a teenager she began to live a very sinful life. Mary's favorite thing was to go to wild parties where she would dance, sing, and act in impure ways. She didn't have any respect for God's commandments which tell us to be pure in mind, heart, and body.

One day Mary decided to go on vacation to the holy city of Jerusalem. For some reason she went to visit the Church of the Holy Sepulcher where the true cross of Jesus was kept. A strange thing happened when she tried to enter the church: she couldn't pass through its doors! Mary tried three more times to walk through the doors but each time a mysterious force kept her from entering. She looked up above the entrance and saw a picture of Our Lady. Suddenly, she was filled with sorrow for her wild life and promised to give up her sinful ways. Then she tried to enter the church once more and was now able to do so. She went to pray before the cross of Our Lord and wept tears of sorrow for her many sins. Upon leaving the church Mary whispered a little prayer by the picture of the Blessed Virgin above the doors and she heard Our Lady's voice saying, "Go out beyond the Jordan River and you will find rest and comfort."

The very next morning Mary went to the Church of St. John the Baptist at the Jordan River. She received the Sacraments of Reconciliation and Holy Eucharist, and then set out to begin her life as a hermitess in the desert. Mary lived in a cave and ate roots, dates, and wild honey for food. Water was her only drink. Her clothes soon fell apart and so she suffered from both the heat and the cold. During these years Mary was often tempted by the pleasures of her past sins, but she always turned to Our Lady to whom she had consecrated her life. She saw and spoke with no one for the next forty-seven years.

About this time their lived a holy monk named Zosimus who used to spend the days of Lent in the desert. On the First Sunday of Lent in the year 430, Zosimus was at prayer in the desert when he saw someone moving about near his cave. The person said to him, "I am a woman. Please give me your cloak so that I can cover myself and we can talk." The woman was Mary of Egypt. She told the holy monk all about her sinful life and of her conversion in Jerusalem. She went to confession to Zosimus and then asked him to bring her the Eucharist on his trip out to the desert the next year. He promised to do so.

True to his word, the monk carried the Eucharist to Mary on Holy Thursday in the year 431. Mary met him at the Jordan, made the sign of the cross over its water and then walked across the river! After praying the Apostle's Creed and the Our Father, she received the Body and Blood of Christ in Holy Communion. She spoke with Zosimus for a while and then returned to her cave.

The next Lent, when Zosimus went to talk with Mary he found that she had died. She had left a note for him which read, "Father Zosimus, please bury the body of lowly Mary and pray for me. I died on the night of the Lord's Passion after receiving the Bread of Life from angels." Zosimus buried Mary's body, took her cloak as a relic, and returned to his monastery. He told everyone about this holy woman of the desert and she soon became honored as a saint by the people. Another monk wrote down Mary's story and so we are able to know all about her today. Byzantine Catholics celebrate her feastday on the First Sunday of Lent and Roman Catholics honor her every year on April 2.

The Priest Who Started Catholic Schools

St. John-Baptist de la Salle — April 7

Did you know that not very long ago there were no Catholic schools and that only the children of rich families were given an education? Did you ever wonder how our Church schools started and why they are so popular? Well, the story of the Catholic schools is also the story of a very interesting saint. His name is Jean-

ST. JOHN-BAPTIST

DE LA SALLE

Baptiste (John Baptist in English) de la Salle. He was a French priest who obeyed these words of Jesus: "Let the little children come to Me, and do not stop them. For to them belongs the Kingdom of Heaven" (*Mt 19:14*).

Born in the town of Rheims, France in the year 1651, John-Baptist's family was both very Catholic and very rich. He was a good student in school and knew, even when he was little, that God wanted him to become a priest. When he was 19, John-Baptist entered the seminary and was ordained a Catholic priest eight years later. Since he was tall, handsome, and smart, everybody thought that the new Fr. John-Baptist would become a very important bishop one day. But God had very different plans for this new priest's life.

At this time in history, there were thousands of very poor families who could not afford to send their children to school. This made both the parents and children sad, but there seemed to be nothing they could do to change the situation. Then one day a man came to see Fr. John-Baptist. This man had a plan: he and Father would start a new kind of school — a *free school* for the poor kids of the parish.

The teachers would be single men without families to support, and would work for free. The parish would give them a place to live and food to eat. He asked Fr. John-Baptist if he would help make this plan come true. Father had a very good heart, but he knew that saying "yes" to this plan would mean a lot of sacrifices in his life. But he also knew that God wanted him to do it. He answered, "yes," because he loved the poor and wanted to help them as much as he could. He sold all of his property and with the money he bought some buildings for the new school and for a home for the teachers.

At first things were very hard, just as Fr. John-Baptist had thought. Then many men came to join the new teachers' group and free Catholic schools were opened all over France. Fr. John-Baptist gave these teachers a special set of rules to help them live good Christian lives. He also gave them a name, the *Brothers of the Christian Schools* or *Christian Brothers* for short. Fr. John-Baptist was the first teacher to make a school Catholic in both name and spirit. He knew that the most important duty of a Catholic school is to teach children the Gospel and how to live as good Catholic Christians. He used to say that if this was not being done, the school should close its doors.

After a life spent in service to children, families, and the schools, Fr. John-Baptist died on Good Friday, April 7, 1719. The Pope declared John-Baptist de la Salle a saint and made him the patron of all Catholic school teachers. The Brothers of the Christian Schools are now the biggest religious order of Brothers in the Church and they have schools all over the world. With them we celebrate the feastday of their founder every year on April 7.

The Smiling Saint of The Handicapped
St. Julie Rose Billiart — April 8

Have you ever known someone who always seemed to be happy? Someone who, even in bad times, always looked at the bright side of life and kept on smiling? Today's saint was one of these joyful people. She lived during difficult times and had a lot of personal suffering but she never lost her cheerful spirit.

ST. JULIE

BILLIART

As a matter of fact, she has been nick-named *The Smiling Saint*. Her name was Julie Rose Billiart.

Julie was born in France on July 12, 1751. She was the sixth of seven children, of whom only three lived on to adulthood. The Billiart family was neither rich nor poor. They owned a little drapery shop and also worked as part-time farmers. Even as a child, little Julie was very friendly and cheerful. She was quite bright and did so well in religion class that her teacher made her the *catechist* or religion teacher for the younger students.

The parish priest was so impressed by Julie's faith that he made her one of his special helpers when she was only 14. Her duties included teaching catechism and taking up the Sunday collection at Mass. Julie grew closer to God through a life of prayer. She attended Mass and received Holy Communion everyday. She had a special love for the Sacred Heart of Jesus and for Mary, our Blessed Mother. When she was 15 years old, Julie made a vow of chastity, promising God that she would remain single so as to belong to Him in a special way. This also allowed her to be freer to serve God's people.

A tragic event took place when Julie was 21. One night, as she and her father were sitting in their living room, someone shot a bullet through the window! No one was hurt, but the horrible shock of this action caused Julie great mental suffering. Because of this she lost the use of her legs. For the next 30 years she was to be handicapped and confined to a wheelchair. Yet Julie never lost her cheerful spirit. She even came up with a motto that went like this, "How good is the good God!" From her wheelchair this brave woman did more work for God and the Church that most people ever even dream of doing.

When she was 38, the French government went through a lot of changes and the new leaders began a persecution of the Church. They arrested and even killed priests who were loyal to the Pope. They bribed other pastors to stop following the leadership of our Holy Father. The leaders put these unfaithful priests in charge of the parishes hoping to lead the people away from the Pope. Julie refused to follow these new pastors and led other Catholics against them, too. She gave food and shelter to the faithful priests and because of this the government wanted her killed. She secretly escaped to the neighboring country of Belgium where God had more work for her to do.

In this new land, Julie met some good Catholic women and together they started a community called the *Sisters of Notre Dame* (which is French for "Our Lady"). Their special work was to teach catechism to children. Julie became their leader and over the years many girls became Notre Dame Sisters. When she was 53, Julie was miraculously cured of her handicap during a novena to the Sacred Heart of Jesus. Now she was able to travel to many more places to open schools and carry out other good works for God's people. But soon after this cure, Julie fell down a flight of stairs and hurt herself very badly. Once again she was unable to move about. Even though she had to stay in bed all day long, she never lost her joyful spirit.

On April 8, 1815, the Smiling Saint died. When people prayed to her for help in their needs many miracles began to take place. The Pope eventually declared her a saint and she is now a patron of catechists. Thousands of young ladies have joined Julie's sisterhood since her death and today the Notre Dame Sisters can be found all over the world. We celebrate the joyful life of St. Julie Rose Billiart every year on April 8.

The Jewel of Heaven
St. Gemma Galgani — April 11

Nobody likes to suffer. It is an awful thing to be sick or to feel sad. But do you know that suffering can become a gift which we offer to God for the good of others? Before Jesus died on the cross suffering was just a horrible thing that human beings tried to avoid. But by accepting sorrow and pain during His Passion, Jesus

turned it into a way to help others reach Heaven. We, too, can learn to accept the sufferings of life in a spirit of love for God and offer it to Him for others. This doesn't mean we should go around looking for ways to suffer. But whenever sadness or pain comes into our lives we don't have to see it as "bad news." We can offer it to Jesus and turn it into "good news" for the salvation of all people. This is what today's saint did her whole life long. She had a lot of sorrows but she accepted them cheerfully, and became a special follower of Christ our Savior.

Gemma Galgani was born in the beautiful northern Italian town of Lucca on March 12, 1878. Her godfather was the one who wanted her named Gemma which means "jewel" in the Italian language. But her mother disagreed since there wasn't a saint named Gemma. The parish priest settled the argument by saying to Mrs. Galgani, "Call her Gemma because she will become a shining jewel of Heaven."

Gemma was the fourth of seven children born in the Galgani family. Her father was a pharmacist and he was very generous to the poor and needy. By the time Gemma was five years old she already knew how to read and write. In school she did very well in her studies and always won the "good conduct" award for her grade. Her love for the Blessed Sacrament was so strong that from the day of her first Holy Communion, she tried never to miss daily Mass.

Her first experience with suffering happened when her mother died. Gemma was only eight years old but she said to her family, "Let's not cry for Mama. Her suffering is over and now she is happy with Jesus in Heaven." More suffering entered her life as a teenager. Both her father and her favorite brother died. Then she caught a strange disease that made her lose both her hearing and all her hair. This lasted for three long years until she was 21 years old. One of her greatest sorrows was to have to be separated from her dear family so that they wouldn't catch her disease. But through it all Gemma never got mad at God or complained of her many pains. She had learned to accept these things as cheerfully as she could and to offer them to Jesus for the salvation of all people.

During this time of suffering a good priest became friends with Gemma. He helped her to grow closer to God by a life of prayer. He was a Passionist Father, a member of a religious community devoted to preaching about the Passion and Cross of Jesus. Gemma decided to become a Passionist, too. But her health was too poor to be accepted as a nun. So she remained a laywoman but followed the Passionist spirit of prayer and penance.

God blessed Gemma with many special spiritual gifts. She had visions of Jesus, Mary, and her Guardian Angel. They told her that her sufferings were really helping other people to know, love, and serve God. How happy this made Gemma feel! But at the same time some people in her town were calling her crazy. They gossiped about Gemma and called her names. Once, they even threw rocks at her while she was walking to Mass!

In 1903, 24-year-old Gemma caught the same disease that had killed her mother so many years before. She accepted this illness just as she had accepted all her pains and offered it as a gift of love to God. On Holy Saturday of that year, Gemma Galgani died. She who loved the cross so much in this world would celebrate the great Resurrection Feast of Easter in Heaven! So many miracles happened when people prayed to her that the Pope declared her a saint in 1940. The Passionist Order and many other Catholics celebrate her feastday on April 11.

The Girl Nobody Wanted

Bl. Margaret of Castello — April 13

Isn't it sad when people make fun of others just because of the way they look, or speak, or walk? Imagine how much it must hurt to be laughed at and to be unwanted by others. The woman whom we are honoring today knew very well how horrible this kind of teasing can be. She was rejected and unwanted even by her own

BLESSED MARGARET

OF CASTELLO

parents because of the way she looked. Yet she rose above her handicap and became one of the most wonderful and holy of Jesus' followers. Her name is Blessed Margaret of Castello.

Margaret was born in Italy to rich and well-known parents in the year 1287. Her parents were so happy to be having a baby that they spread the news far and wide. However, their joy turned to sorrow when their little girl was born. She was deformed and blind, with a bent body and an ugly face. When her father found out about this he ordered the infant to be kept out of sight. He was embarrassed by Margaret's appearance and never spoke a word about her to anyone.

When she was five years old, Margaret was sent away from the family castle and locked up in a little room near a church. She lived there for 12 years all by herself with only a few short visits from her mother. When she was 17 years of age her parents brought her to a shrine in Castello, Italy, hoping that God would cure her there. When a miracle failed to take place she was cruelly abandoned by her mother and father while she was reciting her prayers before the altar. Luckily, the local villagers felt sorry for the poor girl. They took her into their homes and made her feel welcome for the first time in her short life.

Even though Margaret had many bodily problems she was very smart and also very holy. She had deep faith, hope, and love for God. Never once did she complain about her sufferings. Nor did she speak an unkind word about the parents who had abandoned her. Instead, Margaret looked at the bright side of things and always tried to make life a bit happier for those around her. She had a great love for the Holy Eucharist and a special devotion to the Holy Family of Jesus, Mary, and Joseph.

When she was a teenager Margaret joined the Third Order of St. Dominic. She was the very first unmarried woman to belong to this lay community. Dressed in the white Dominican robes, Margaret hobbled about the village caring for the sick, visiting prisoners, and helping everyone in need. God blessed her with the gift of working miracles which she used to help those who were suffering and dying. Margaret even started a day-care center at her home for the local children where she taught them catechism and had lots of fun playing games.

Margaret died at 33 years of age in the year 1320. The girl whom nobody wanted at first, had been adopted by a whole town and was sadly missed by everyone in it. They buried her with great honors in the church where she had been abandoned sixteen years earlier. So many miracles took place at her tomb that the Pope declared her Blessed. Margaret is a good reminder to us today that it doesn't matter at all if a person is beautiful or ugly, fat or thin, healthy or sick. What counts is that we love God with all our hearts and live our lives according to the teachings of Jesus. In our times, when many people turn to abortion to destroy the life of an unwanted unborn child, Blessed Margaret of Castello is honored as a patroness of the pro-life movement. The Dominicans celebrate her feastday on April 13.

The Beautiful Lady and The Little Girl
St. Bernadette Soubirous — April 16

ST. BERNADETTE

AND OUR LADY

Even though God took the Blessed Virgin Mary to Heaven body and soul, she has returned to earth on a number of occasions in visions or apparitions to various people. One of these special visits of Mary happened in the little town of Lourdes, France, in the year 1858. From February 11 to July 16 of that year, our Blessed Mother appeared 18 times to a 14-year-old girl named Bernadette Soubirous.

Bernadette was a very sickly child and her family was the poorest one in the whole town. They lived in an old rundown, falling-apart building that used to be the city jail. Her father couldn't always find work so quite often the Soubirous family didn't have enough food to eat.

One cold day in February, the family was out of firewood, so Bernadette and her little sister went out to the woods to gather some twigs. During this outing, Bernadette looked up at a grotto or cave where she suddenly saw a circle of white light. Inside the light was the most beautiful woman she had ever seen! The Lady was dressed all in white with a bright blue sash and a long white veil covering her hair. She held a shiny pearl rosary in her hands and there were golden roses over each foot! Bernadette was a bit afraid, so she took out the little rosary which she always carried in her pocket and began to say her prayers. This made the Lady very happy!

When they got home, Bernadette found out that her little sister hadn't seen a thing. Her mother thought that she was lying about the Lady so she punished Bernadette. Soon, the story of the Beautiful Lady spread all over the town and most everyone made fun of the little girl. Poor Bernadette! She knew that she had really seen a most beautiful Lady at the grotto. She returned to this cave almost everyday and the Lady appeared to her 17 more times. She spoke to Bernadette about God and of how important it was for people to love and pray to Him with all their hearts. She told Bernadette to remind everyone of the need to do penance to show that they are sorry for their sins. She also asked the priests to build a church in Lourdes and promised to make it a special place.

One day, when Bernadette asked the Lady her name she said, "I am the Immaculate Conception." This meant that she was the most pure and holy Mother of God. Now the priests and people knew that it really was the Blessed Virgin who had come to Lourdes! Then Mary made a miraculous spring of water flow from the soil. Many who drank this water or used it to wash their wounds experienced healings and other miracles! The Bishop studied all about these visions of Our Lady and then declared them to be true. He had a big church (called a *basilica*) built in Lourdes at the spot where the Blessed Virgin Mary had appeared, and people came from all over the world to visit this holy place. Even today, almost 150 years later, about 10,000 people — especially the sick — visit Lourdes everyday and many are cured there.

When Bernadette was older, she decided to become a nun. She joined the Sisters of Charity and Christian Instruction who had been her catechism teachers when she was a little girl. Her new name was Sister Marie-Bernarde and she served God as a nurse, taking care of the sick nuns who lived in her convent. People often came to the convent wanting to talk to her, but Sister Marie-Bernarde preferred to be left alone. She didn't think that she was a very important person. When she was 35 years old, Sister Marie-Bernarde became very ill. She remembered what Our Lady of Lourdes had told her when she was a little girl, "I cannot promise to make you happy on earth, but I will make you happy forever in Heaven." She died within the year on April 16, 1879. The Pope declared Bernadette Soubirous a saint in 1925 and set her feast for April 16. The Church also celebrates the visions of Our Lady of Lourdes every year on February 11.

The Secretary of the First Pope
St. Mark the Evangelist — April 25

very Sunday at Mass Catholics listen to a reading from one of the four Gospels. These Gospels are holy books written by men with the help of the Holy Spirit. From the Gospels we learn what Jesus really did and said while He lived on earth. Those who wrote the Gospels are called *evangelists*. Today's saint was one of these special men. His name was Mark.

Mark, who is also called John Mark in the New Testament, was born in Jerusalem. His mother was one of the first Christians of this city and, together with a few other women disciples, she used to help care for Jesus and His Apostles. Mark was a young man when Jesus lived and after the Resurrection, he became a companion of the great missionaries, Sts. Paul and Barnabas (who was his cousin). With them he helped to spread the Good News about Jesus among the peoples of various lands.

When St. Paul was arrested and brought to Rome for trial, Mark stayed with him to help him in many ways. He also helped St. Peter, the first Pope, and became his secretary. Mark wrote down the many memories which this Apostle had of Jesus and these writings became the *Gospel of St. Mark*. Mark's is the shortest and easiest to read of the four Gospels. It shows us what events and sayings of Jesus were used to instruct new Christians in the Faith.

After the coming of the Holy Spirit on Pentecost Sunday, Mark was made a bishop by the Apostles and sent to preach the Good News in the city of Alexandria, Egypt. He baptized many converts, ordained men as priests, and soon Alexandria became an important Christian community. When the Egyptian ruler started a persecution of Christians, Mark was arrested and thrown into prison. The holy bishop was tied up with ropes and dragged over a road of sharp stones. In this way he died as a martyr for Christ. St. Mark the Evangelist is honored every year on his feastday of April 25.

A Special Woman with a Special Mission
St. Catherine of Siena — April 29

T he Bible tells us that whenever God wants to do a special work, He uses very ordinary people to carry out His plans. In the New Testament God chose Mary, a poor Jewish girl, to become Mother of the Savior. He selected Mary Magdalen, who had been an unwanted public sinner, to become the *Apostle to the Apostles* with the Good News of the Resurrection. Today's saint, Catherine of Siena, was one of these ordinary people with an extraordinary job to do for God. It was her mission to "wake up" the Church during a "sleepy time" in its long history.

ST. CATHERINE

OF SIENA, T.O.P.

Catherine Benincasa was born on March 25, 1347, as a twin and the 24th child in her family. At the time of her birth, the world was a very confusing and mixed-up place. A horrible disease called the Black Plague was killing thousands of people everywhere. Cities and countries were always at war with one another. Even the Church was in trouble because the Pope had left the city of Rome and moved to France. This was bad news to the Christians because St. Peter, the first Pope, had made Rome the headquarters of the Church and everyone expected the Pope to live there. They were angry that he moved away and many stopped obeying him because of it.

Catherine was a very beautiful girl with long golden hair. She was so pretty that many young men wanted to marry her. But Catherine had already promised to live for Jesus in a special way. She didn't want to get married or become a nun. Instead, she became a Dominican tertiary. A *tertiary* is a layperson who promises to live a life of simplicity, purity and obedience while living in the world according to the spirit of a religious order without becoming a priest or nun. Today Dominican tertiaries are called *Lay Dominicans*. Catherine began to pray more and to take care of the sick and needy. The poor people loved her and would follow her everywhere.

One night, while everyone in the house was asleep, Jesus appeared to Catherine in a vision and placed a beautiful ring upon her finger. The ring was a sign that He loved her as a special friend. It was at this time that Catherine received her special mission: to bring the Holy Father back to Rome and to teach Catholics to honor and obey him. This was a very big job for a young woman who was only 20 years old! Many people laughed at Catherine and called her crazy. Some even tried to kill her. But God started working miracles through her prayers to show that she was His messenger and friend. Soon the people stopped making fun of Catherine and began listening to her words.

Catherine had great respect for the Pope and called him the *sweet Christ upon earth*. As the weeks and months went by, she wrote many letters to the Holy Father, begging him to return to Rome. Catherine asked him to be a strong leader of God's people who were suffering in so many ways. Finally, the Pope obeyed the voice of God, speaking through the words of His servant, Catherine. He moved back to St. Peter's city of Rome. How happy Catherine was to have fulfilled the mission given to her by God!

Now that she had carried out her special work, Catherine felt that her life on earth was soon to end. She died when she was only 33 years old. Soon afterwards, the Holy Father declared her to be a saint. He made her the patroness of the Church and heavenly helper of the Popes. Because of her love and care for the sick she is also the patroness of nurses. We celebrate her feastday on April 29.

Two Special Friends of Jesus

St. Philip the Apostle — May 3   St. James the Less — May 3

Do you remember the Bible story about the choosing of the Twelve Apostles of Jesus? When Our Lord was about 30 years old, He picked twelve men to help Him teach others about God and how to live as children of our heavenly Father. He called these men *apostles*, which means, "those who are sent out on a mission." Philip and James the Less are two of these specially chosen followers of Christ.

St. Philip the Apostle

Philip was born in the town of Bethsaida of Galilee, which is very close to the town where Jesus lived as a boy. He was a friend of Jesus' cousin, St. John the Baptist, and that was how he came to meet Our Lord. He was married and had three daughters who dedicated their lives to serving God and spreading the Good News among the people.

St. Philip is mentioned a lot in the Bible. In the Gospel of St. John we learn that Philip brought a friend (Nathanael) to meet Jesus and that he helped feed the people when Jesus worked the miracle of the loaves and fishes. At the Last Supper, he asked Jesus to tell us more about God the Father. After the Resurrection of the Lord, Philip went to other lands to tell people about the Good News of Jesus. Like the other Apostles, he was *martyred* or killed for his Christian Faith. Some men nailed him to a cross and so he died like Jesus. This is why pictures of St. Philip the Apostle usually show him holding a small cross.

55

St. James the Less

There were two Apostles named James. To tell the difference between them, the older one is called St. James the Greater, and the younger James is nicknamed "the Less." James the Less is the one we are celebrating today. His mother was a relative of the Blessed Virgin Mary and so James and Jesus were cousins. Jewish people used to call relatives and even good friends "brothers" and so sometimes in the Bible James is called the "brother of the Lord."

After Jesus rose from the dead and returned to Heaven, James became the first Bishop of Jerusalem. This was the second most important job in the Church. Do you know who had the most important work? Peter, the Apostle who became the first Pope and leader of the Christians. James is also special to us because he wrote one of the *epistles* or letters which are in the New Testament. It is from the Letter of St. James in the Bible that we learn about the sacrament Jesus gave us which is called Anointing of the Sick (see *Jm 5:14-15*). This sacrament is meant to help those who are very sick or who are dying. It brings the grace and peace of Our Lord Jesus Christ to those who are ill and gives them strength to be patient in their sufferings. In this letter St. James also reminds us to show our faith by doing good works for the poor. St. James the Less was martyred in Jerusalem in the year 62. Like St. Stephen, who was the very first Christian martyr, James was stoned to death while praying for his enemies. We celebrate the feastday of the Apostles Philip and James the Less on May 3.

The Sister Who Served Christ in His Priests
Bl. Marie-Leonie Paradis — May 3

BL. MARIE

LEONIE PARADIS

Do you remember the Bible story about Martha and Mary? They were the two sisters of Lazarus whom Jesus raised from the dead. They lived in the town of Bethany and Jesus used to go to their house whenever He was in that village. Martha would cook delicious meals for Our Lord and His companions while Mary loved to sit at His feet to hear more about the Good News. The holy woman we are honoring today was very much like Sts. Martha and Mary. She dedicated her life to taking care of priests just as the two sisters of Bethany took care of Jesus and the Apostles. Her name is Blessed Marie-Leonie Paradis.

Elodie Paradis was born in French Canada on May 12, 1840. Her parents were good Catholic Christians who taught Elodie and her five brothers to love God above all things. Mrs. Paradis was a very kind and charitable woman whose tender love for the needy touched the heart of her little daughter. Following her mother's good example, Elodie had a special love for the poor and always tried to make others happy.

When she was 10 years old, Elodie was sent to live at a convent school run by the Notre Dame Sisters. At first she was very homesick but after a while she grew to enjoy her life at school. She was especially fond of the nuns who taught her so many wonderful things. Impressed by their holy lives, Elodie decided that she, too, would become a Sister one day.

Elodie joined the Holy Cross Sisters when she was almost 14 years old. She received the religious name of Marie-Leonie and was sent to teach at a school for girls. Sister Marie-Leonie enjoyed her work as a teacher but deep inside her heart she had a secret desire to serve Jesus by taking care of His priests. She thought of how Our Lady took care of Jesus in Nazareth, and of the holy women in the Gospel stories who cared for Our Lord and His Twelve Apostles. Sister Marie-Leonie asked God to show her the way to make this dream come true. Her prayers were answered when she was sent to the United States to help take care of the Holy Cross priests at Notre Dame University in Indiana.

In 1880, together with a few companions, Mother Marie-Leonie, as she was now called, founded a new religious community called the *Little Sisters of the Holy Family*. Their special work was to serve priests and take care of them just as they would take care of Jesus Himself. The Little Sisters found great joy in cooking, cleaning, and doing many other things which needed to be done in the priest's rectories and seminaries. Mother Marie-Leonie passed on to her community her great love for the Holy Eucharist, for our Blessed Mother and the rosary. She reminded the Little Sisters that their many household works freed the priests to carry out their wonderful mission of love and service among God's people.

Over the years hundreds of women became Little Sisters of the Holy Family and the community spread across Canada and the United States. Mother Marie-Leonie often visited the many different convents of the community. She would speak to the Sisters about how close priests are to the heart of Our Lord and how they continue His saving work upon earth. Like Jesus, His priests change bread and wine into His Body and Blood at Mass, they forgive sins through the Sacrament of Reconciliation, and preach the Good News for all to hear. She taught the Little Sisters to pray always and to offer their lives that all priests may become holy servants of the Lord.

Mother Marie-Leonie was the leader of the Little Sisters until the day she died, May 3, 1912. After her death God worked many miracles for those who prayed to her and in 1984, Pope John Paul II declared her a Blessed of the Church. Today there are over 700 Little Sisters of the Holy Family serving Jesus and His priests in Canada, the U.S.A., Italy, and Central America. The feastday of Blessed Marie-Leonie Paradis is celebrated by the Little Sisters and by Catholics in Canada on May 3.

The Teenage Saint of Turin
St. Dominic Savio — May 6

Many people feel that teenage boys are just about the most mischievous people in the whole world! They think that all these boys use bad language, get into fights, and cause all kinds of trouble. Maybe some of them do these things, but others can be very good and brave young men. Today's saint was a normal fun-loving teenager. He used all his youthful energy and enthusiasm to do good and he has become one of the most popular saints of the Church. His name is Dominic Savio.

SAINT DOMINIC

TO CHOOSE DEATH OVER SIN.

◆ SAVIO ◆

Dominic was born near Piedmont, Italy on April 2, 1842. His family was poor and his Dad worked as a blacksmith in their little town. Dominic was always a good boy, obedient to his parents and respectful of his elders. His love for the Mass was so great that he became an altar boy when he was only five years old, and from the age of six he wanted to grow up to become a priest.

On his First Holy Communion Day Dominic made these four promises to God which he always kept: (1) To go to Confession and Holy Communion often. (2) To honor Sundays and Holy Days of Obligation as special times of worship and rest. (3) To have Jesus and Mary as his best friends. (4) To choose death over sin. This fourth promise was very special. Dominic knew that *mortal* or serious sins destroy God's life in our souls and closes the gates of Heaven to us. He knew that mortal sin is worse than dying.

When Dominic was 12 years old a holy priest, St. John Bosco, opened a boarding school for boys in the nearby city of Turin. Dominic enrolled in this school and quickly became the most popular of all the students. He was never rude or mean to the others but always tried to be helpful and polite. He started a new club at school called the *Sodality of the Immaculate Conception*. Its members were boys who wanted to live good Catholic lives and who volunteered to help their fellow students in various ways.

After three years, Dominic's happy life at school came to an end. He had become very sick and was sent home so that his parents could take care of him. His friends and teachers were all sad to see him go, but they hoped that he would return to them soon. That, however, was not meant to be.

On March 9, 1857, Dominic died while having a vision of Heaven. His last words were, "What beautiful things I see!" He was just one month short of his 15th birthday. About one hundred years later, in 1954, Dominic Savio was proclaimed a saint by the Holy Father. He is the patron of choir singers and of teenage boys. In many Catholic schools today, especially those run by the Salesian Order of St. John Bosco, there are *Savio Clubs* whose members take the teenage Saint of Turin as their model. They celebrate the feast of St. Dominic Savio every year on May 6.

The Flower of the Holy Eucharist

Bl. Imelda Lambertini — May 13

O ne of the most wonderful memories of growing up Catholic is the day of First Holy Communion. Dressed in beautiful white dresses with veils, or in fancy shirts with grownup ties, the happy children are filled with excitement and joy as they approach the altar to receive the Body and Blood of Christ for the very

BLESSED

IMELDA

first time! Today's story is about a marvelous little girl who loved the Blessed Sacrament so dearly that she has become known as the *Flower of the Holy Eucharist* and the patroness of First Communicants. Her name is Blessed Imelda Lambertini.

Imelda was born in the beautiful and historic city of Bologna, Italy, in the year 1322. The Lambertinis were one of the town's richest and most powerful families. They were also very good Catholics who supported many works of the Church. Some of their relatives included famous bishops, nuns, and even one of the Holy Fathers, Pope Benedict XIV.

As a little girl Imelda used to go with her mother to Mass every day. Afterwards they would visit the sick and help the needy. She loved to set up little shrines in her home where she would place a picture of Jesus and Mary and which she decorated with colorful wild flowers collected from the fields. Here she would offer her daily prayers, especially the Psalms from the Old Testament of the Bible.

When she was nine years old, Imelda went to live at a nearby monastery of Dominican nuns where she attended the convent school and took part in the daily prayers of the Sisters. She was loved very much by the nuns who praised her for her purity, joyfulness, and obedience. Imelda was so very happy at the monastery but one thing did cause her a bit of sorrow. Imelda had a deep love for the Real Presence of Jesus at Mass and in the tabernacle, but she was not old enough to receive the Eucharist. In those days children had to be at least 12 years old before making their First Holy Communion. She used to say to the Sisters, "How can anyone receive Jesus into their hearts and not die from this great joy?"

When she was 11 years old Imelda's great wish to receive the Blessed Sacrament came true. But it was to be both her first and last Holy Communion. On May 12, 1333, which was the feast of the Ascension of Jesus that year, all the community gathered for Mass and afterwards went about their daily duties. Imelda remained alone in the chapel kneeling in front of the tabernacle where she told Jesus of her great wish to receive Him. Suddenly, a consecrated host appeared above her head and a great light, as bright as the sun, filled the room. It attracted the attention of the priest and Sisters who came running to see what had happened. When he saw the host miraculously floating above Imelda's head, the priest reverently took it into his hands and gave the little girl her First Communion. Imelda smiled with great joy, crossed her arms over her breast, and collapsed upon the floor. When the nuns went to lift her up they discovered that she had died. Her prayers had been answered and Imelda had gone straight to Heaven after making her First Holy Communion.

Many miracles took place when people prayed to this Flower of the Eucharist and later the Holy Father declared her a Blessed. She is one of the youngest Catholics to be so honored by the Church. The life of Blessed Imelda reminds us to always receive Jesus with pure hearts and to be respectful and prayerful in church. She is a good model for Catholics of every age and especially for those who are preparing to make their own First Holy Communion. Her feastday is celebrated by the Dominican Order every year on May 13.

The Last But Not Least of the Apostles
St. Matthias the Apostle — May 14

Did you ever feel kind of "left out" because you were not chosen to be on a team? Or have you ever felt a little sad because you were chosen very last to be on the team? If you have, then St. Matthias is your special heavenly friend. He was chosen last to be on the team of Jesus' Twelve Apostles, but his life reminds us that being last does not mean being the least!

ST. MATTHIAS

They chose another to take his place. Acts 1: 26

APOSTLE of JESUS

Do you remember that Jesus picked twelve men to share in His mission to teach the people the truth about God and religion? These men, called the Twelve Apostles, were specially taught by Jesus Who explained many things to them. At the Last Supper Jesus made them the first Catholic priests. After the Resurrection, Christ gave them orders to go out to all the world preaching the Good News and celebrating the sacraments. Our Lord made these men the very first *bishops* or leaders of the Church. Our bishops today carry on the same works as the Twelve Apostles. They have the same share in Christ's power and mission as the first Apostles did. This is why we call our bishops the *successors of the Apostles.*

Jesus chose these men from among a group of seventy-two helpers. Matthias was one of these helpers but he was not chosen to be one of the Apostles. A few years later, one of the Twelve Apostles, Judas Iscariot, did a horrible thing. He helped the soldiers capture Jesus! Even though Jesus forgave His betrayer, Judas did another terrible thing. He killed himself! After Christ rose from the dead and returned to Heaven, the eleven remaining Apostles met together in the city of Jerusalem. They knew that Jesus had wanted twelve special helpers to preach the Good News so they decided to choose someone to take Judas' place. After praying for help in making the right decision, they elected Matthias as the new Apostle. Matthias didn't mind that he wasn't chosen the first time, and he didn't care that he was picked very last this time. He was just so happy and honored to become one of the special Twelve Apostles of the Lord!

On the day of Pentecost the Holy Spirit came down upon the followers of Jesus. He filled their hearts with the fire of His love and made them brave in preaching about Our Savior. When the Apostles went out to different lands to spread the Good News of salvation, Matthias traveled to the country of Greece. By the power of God he worked many great miracles among the people there. He cured the sick, gave sight to the blind, and helped the poor in many ways. Like the other Apostles, Matthias baptized new Christians and ordained men to serve as priests.

Even though many of the Greeks loved and listened to Matthias, there were some who did not like him or his preaching about Jesus. One day, they captured Matthias and nailed him to a cross just as the soldiers had done to Christ. He died as a martyr for the Faith as did the other eleven helpers of the Lord. We celebrate the feast of St. Matthias the Apostle every year on May 14.

The Holy Brother of Spain
St. Paschal Baylon — May 17

O n the night before He died, Jesus gave us a most special gift, the gift of Himself in the Holy Eucharist. The Eucharist is also called the *Blessed Sacrament* because in it Jesus is among us in a most wonderful and special way. When the priest offers Mass and says the words which Jesus spoke at the Last Supper,

"This is My Body.... This is the cup of My Blood...," the consecrated bread and wine become the Body and Blood of Christ, food and drink for our souls. This is why the saints have all called the Mass the greatest prayer of Christians. Today's saint was very devoted to the Mass and Blessed Sacrament. His name was Paschal Baylon.

Paschal (whose name means "Easter") was born in Spain in the year 1540. The Baylon family was so poor that Paschal was not able to go to school. Instead, he worked as a shepherd boy. Paschal loved this work because it gave him a lot of time for playing, thinking, and praying. He was very smart and while watching the sheep Paschal taught himself how to read. After making his First Holy Communion, he made every effort to attend Mass and receive the Body of Christ everyday. He also loved Mary our Blessed Mother very much and prayed the rosary daily while taking care of the sheep.

A most wonderful thing happened to Paschal when he was a teenager. Some mean shepherds who were jealous of his goodness tried to keep him from attending Mass. They blocked the road to the church and wouldn't let him pass. Do you know what God did to help His friend? He sent an angel to the fields with the Holy Eucharist and Paschal received the Body and Blood of Christ from him! This true story was witnessed by some of the mean shepherds and they never bothered Paschal again.

When Paschal was a bit older he decided to dedicate his whole life to God as a Brother in the Franciscan Order. A *Brother* is a man who makes special promises to God to live a holy life and to serve the Church as a member of a religious community. Brother Paschal served God by taking care of the buildings where he lived and by welcoming all who came as pilgrims to the parish church. He would chat with the visitors and listen to their problems. He always promised to remember their needs when he prayed before the Blessed Sacrament.

Soon the people began calling Paschal the *Holy Brother* because God seemed to work through him in special ways. He received the gift of curing the sick and one time he even saved the life of a little boy who was dying. As news of the Holy Brother spread, visitors from all over the land began to come to his church and ask his prayers. Paschal told all his visitors to go and pray before Our Lord in the tabernacle and tell Him their needs. He would speak to them of the great love which Jesus has for everyone and of how the Lord delights in having us visit Him in the Blessed Sacrament.

Brother Paschal Baylon died when he was 52 years old. Even from Heaven he kept helping those who prayed to him. The Holy Father declared Paschal to be a saint and made him the heavenly helper of all those who wish to grow deeper in their love for the Holy Eucharist. We celebrate the feast of this good follower of Jesus on May 17.

The Helper of the Hopeless
St. Rita of Cascia — May 22

SAINT RITA

OF CASCIA

I n fairy tales like Cinderella, whenever a man and woman get married they "live happily ever after." But real life is not always like that. Sometimes a husband and wife do not live happily ever after at all. How sad this is, but it's true. St. Rita of Cascia is a special heavenly friend and helper of these people.

Margarita Mancini was born in the town of Cascia, Italy on May 22, 1381. Her parents had prayed to God for a long time for the gift of a baby. So when little Rita (which they called her for short) was born they were so very happy! Rita was a lively girl who liked animals and had all kinds of pets: chickens, goats, rabbits, and geese. She used to help her mother a lot, especially by cooking and sewing clothes.

When she was 12, which was considered a grown-up age way back then, Rita decided to become a nun so that she could serve God and His people in a special way. But in those days girls had to become what their parents wanted them to be, and the Mancinis wanted Rita to get married. She obeyed and became the wife of Paolo Ferdinando, one of Cascia's most popular and handsome young men. They soon had two sons and were at first a very happy family. But then Paolo began to change. He would yell a lot at Rita and once he even hit her! As the boys grew older they followed their Dad's bad example and poor Rita had many years of family troubles. But she loved her husband and sons and did not give up on them. She prayed a lot for them to

67

become better men and found strength by going to daily Mass and receiving Holy Communion. Rita remembered that Jesus suffered for us on the cross and offered His sufferings to God the Father for the forgiveness of sins. So she offered up her sufferings to God as well.

One day Paolo finally did change for the better. This is how it happened. He came home in a bad mood and started to yell as usual. Then, when he raised up a hand to slap his wife, she grabbed and kissed it! Suddenly Paolo began to cry and said he was sorry for the way he had treated his wife in the past, and from that day on he lived a good Christian life. However, sad events soon interrupted the Ferdinando family's newfound happiness. Paolo was killed one night by a group of men, and soon after this the two boys died of horrible illnesses. Rita was 40 years old at this time and decided to make her childhood dream of being a nun finally come true.

She went to the local convent of Augustinian Nuns and asked to be accepted as a member of the community. At first the Mother Superior said "no" because she thought that Rita was too old to become a nun. But Rita did not give up. She prayed a lot that the Superior would change her mind and that is exactly what happened. In her new life as a nun, Sister Rita would help the other Sisters and used to spend many hours praying before the crucifix in their chapel. She had a great devotion to the Passion, which refers to Jesus' carrying of the cross and crucifixion on Mount Calvary. One time Jesus appeared to her with a crown of thorns upon His head. He thanked her for her prayers in honor of His Passion. Then one of the thorns came off the crown and touched her on the forehead. It left a little mark there as a sign of Rita's love for Jesus and of her prayers for the salvation of all people.

Sister Rita lived in the convent for 36 years. During this time many people came to ask her prayers because she was so holy and close to God. Quite often the sick would be cured and the troubled would find help through her prayers. Sister Rita died on her 76th birthday, May 22, 1457. People came from all over Italy to attend her funeral and to ask her help now that she was in Heaven. The Pope declared Rita an official saint of the Church and the patron or helper of persons in desperate situations. Even today many Catholics say that St. Rita always helps them by her prayers. We celebrate the feast of this wonderful woman every year on May 22.

The Joyful Priest of Rome

St. Philip Neri — May 26

S ometimes you may meet people who think that religion is sup-
posed to be a very somber thing. They don't feel that someone can be a Christian and still have lots of fun! These people
are very wrong! The Bible tells us that one of the special signs of a
holy Christian is joy. *Joy* means that our hearts are happy and full of

gladness in both good times and bad.
Today's saint was nicknamed the *Joyful Saint* for he always tried to bring
happiness into the lives of those he
met. His name was Philip Neri.

Philip was born in Florence, Italy
in 1515. He had a very sad childhood
for someone who was to grow up to
become the Saint of Joy. His mother
died when he was little; his father
asked him to leave home when he
was 18; and an uncle with whom he
hoped to live didn't really want Philip
around at all. He made his way to the
great city of Rome where he found
work as a tutor and spent many hours
visiting the sick in a hospital for the
incurably ill. In his spare time Philip
studied all about God and thought of
ways that he could bring the Good
News to the people of Rome.

At this time in history, most
priests gave sermons that were very
gloomy and sad. They spoke only
about what was wrong with the world
and of how most people were going
to go to Hell because of their sins.
Philip knew that people sin, but he
also knew that everyone has something good in them, too. He began to
speak about how good God the Father is and of Jesus' great love for us
sinners. Philip had a special devotion

to the Holy Spirit Who brings the love of God into our hearts, and he prayed to Him often.

When he was 34 years old, Philip became a priest and gathered around him a little company of young men who used to meet with him every Sunday for prayer and good works. They weren't a religious order but simply a group of friends who wanted to become holy. They called themselves the *Oratory* which means a place of prayer. Some of the members of the group also became priests and together with Fr. Philip they formed a new kind of priestly community called the *Oratorians*. Their special work was to help people live good Christian lives of prayer and service to others.

God gave Fr. Philip some very special gifts such as visions of Our Lady, the power to work miracles, and the grace to read people's minds in the Sacrament of Reconciliation. These gifts, along with his joyful spirit, helped him to become a very popular priest among the people. But he never lost his love of laughter. Fr. Philip would play tricks on people, tell funny jokes, and do lots of things to make others happy.

The Joyful Priest of Rome went on living his holy and happy life until he died in 1595 at the age of 80. Not very long afterwards the Holy Father declared him a saint. Today the priests of the Oratory carry on St. Philip Neri's work of spreading the Good News in the world. With them we celebrate his feastday every year on May 26.

The Girl Who Saved France

St. Joan of Arc — May 30

Not very long ago girls did not have many choices of what to become when they grew up. They could either get married and have a family or become nuns in a monastery. Today's saint was very unusual because God called her to become something which only men were allowed to do in her times. She was to be the

commander of the French army in their battle against England! Her name is St. Joan of Arc, the Patroness and Heroine of France.

Joan was born in the little village of Domremy, France, on January 6, 1412. Her family lived on a farm where Joan spent most of her days shepherding sheep and seeing to many other chores. As a little girl she loved to pray and to help the needy. One time she freely gave up her own bed so that a sick and poor traveler could be taken care of in comfort. Everyone in the village loved Joan because she was so good.

At this time in France the armies of England were invading the country and had taken over much of the land. Suffering and bloodshed were found everywhere because the war had been going on for almost 100 years! The French people were in danger of losing their homes and they begged God to send them the blessing of peace. It was a horrible time in their history.

God answered their prayers in the village of Domremy when Joan was 14 years old. One day while she was out in the garden she began to hear the voices of St. Michael the Archangel, St. Margaret, and St.

Catherine. They were telling her that she had been chosen by God to save France and bring an end to the war. Joan said to them, "I am but a poor peasant girl. I do not even know how to ride or fight in battle." The heavenly visitors replied, "That does not matter. It is God Who wills it." From that day on whenever Joan became afraid or unsure of her plans she would whisper those encouraging words, "God wills it." She knew that the Lord gives us the strength to carry out whatever He asks of us.

You can imagine how the people must have laughed at Joan when they first found out about her voices and her special mission. But after many months, she was able to convince the Crown Prince of France that she was truly chosen by God. He gave her a large army and a shining sword as a sign of his approval. Joan had a beautiful banner made that she always carried into battle. It had a picture of God the Father on it along with the Holy Names of Jesus and Mary. This banner reminded everyone that God had made Joan His holy servant. To protect herself from the enemy Joan cut her hair short and wore men's clothing so that she would appear to be like every other soldier.

For several months Joan and her troops won battle after battle. They drove the English out of many parts of France and rejoiced to see the Crown Prince become the ruler of the land once again. All of France cheered her and praised God for having come to the help of His French people. Then, in the year 1430, a few traitors captured Joan and sold her to the English! Sadly, the French king did nothing to try and save her. After many months in prison she was sentenced to death.

At eight o'clock on the morning of May 30, 1431, Joan was burned at the stake. She was just 19 years old. While the flames leaped up around her, a priest held a crucifix for her to see and she died with the Holy Name of Jesus upon her lips. In 1920, the Holy Father declared Joan of Arc a saint and made her the patroness of France. Her feastday is celebrated with great joy by French Catholics all over the world on May 30.

Heroes of God in Africa
St. Charles Lwanga and Companions — June 3

In what part of the world do you think that the Catholic Church is growing most quickly in membership? Perhaps in Italy where the Pope lives? Or maybe in the United States where we have so many different kinds of people? No. More people are becoming Catholic Christians in Africa than anywhere else in the whole world.

There is an old Christian saying that goes like this: "The blood of martyrs is the seed of Christians." This means that wherever Catholics have died for the Faith the Church will spread and grow. The present day faith of African Catholics has come from the brave Martyrs of Uganda. There were 22 of them, all men or boys between the ages of 13 and 50. This is the true story of their faith, courage, and love.

In the 1880's, French priests went as missionaries to the various lands of Africa to bring the Good New of Jesus to the people who lived there. The native Africans were pagans. They did not know about the one true God but worshipped many false gods like the sun, the water, and certain animals. A number of them listened to the priests and were baptized. It was very difficult to be an African Catholic because many of the rulers of the land did not like this new religion.

The Christians of the Ganda tribe in the kingdom of Buganda (now known as the country of Uganda) were especially in danger. Their *kabaka* (king) was an 18-year-old man named Mwanga. He lived a very wicked life and expected his servants to live sinful lives as well. When

73

many of his servants became Christians they stopped going to the king's parties. They refused to give into the king's sinful desires against the virtue of purity and the commandments of God. During these parties the Christian servants would pray for their king's conversion and instruct other Gandas in the teachings of the Catholic Faith. This made the king very angry and he ordered that all *those who pray* (the Ganda name for Christians) be thrown into jail. They had to make a choice: be faithful to Christ and die, or be faithful to the evil king and live. They all chose Jesus!

While in prison the leader of the servants, Charles Lwanga, encouraged his friends to think about Heaven where they would live forever and ever. He reminded them that Jesus suffered and was crucified for us. He told them that those who die for their faith in Jesus go straight to Heaven to be happy with Him always. These thoughts and their many prayers helped Charles and his companions remain brave and faithful to God.

Once the king heard of the servants' decision to follow Jesus always, he ordered that they be killed. They were marched many miles through the land so that the people could make fun of them and throw stones at them. The prisoners didn't complain. They thought of how Jesus had to walk the way of the cross through the streets of Jerusalem. Finally, they reached the village where they were to be killed. Some of them were pierced with spears while others were burned in a great fire. But all of them died with the Holy Name of Jesus upon their lips. The youngest martyr, Kizito, who was 13, died smiling because he said he was happy to live forever with Our Lord. This happened in the year 1887. In 1964, Pope Paul VI declared these 22 Martyrs of Uganda to be saints of the Catholic Church. We celebrate their feastday on June 3.

The Holy Wife and Mother of Rome
Bl. Anna Maria Taigi — June 9

BLESSED

Anna MARIA

There once lived in the city of Rome a very good Christian who had received the most wondrous gifts from God. This Catholic was so holy that even the Pope would ask this person's advice before making certain decisions. What kind of saint do you think this person was? Maybe a very wise teacher who had studied about God for many years? Or perhaps a priest who spent many hours in prayer? No. This person was a simple Roman wife and mother of a large family. Her name was Anna Maria Taigi and this is the story of her life.

Anna Maria was born in the town of Siena, Italy but her family moved to Rome when she was a little girl. She went to Catholic school until she was 13. At that time she had to go to work because her family was very poor and they needed the extra money to buy food and clothing. Anna Maria was a very beautiful girl with long brown hair and a bright smile. Many young men wanted to marry her but she had already decided on one: Dominic Taigi. When they met it was love at first sight! They were both poor but that didn't matter because they knew that love, not money, is what makes a marriage good and happy. Dominic and Anna were married in 1790 when she was 20 years old.

At first, Anna was more interested in parties, fine dresses, and fancy jewelry than in living a holy Christian life. There's nothing wrong with these things, of course, but if we pay more attention to them than we do to God, then something is wrong and we need to change. Anna's change came when she went to confession to a holy priest. He helped Anna to decide to become a saint! Afterwards she started thinking more about God and spent extra time in prayer each day. She became a lay member of the Trinitarian religious order and carried out many good works for the poor and needy.

The Taigis had seven children and a very happy family life. Every night after the family rosary, both parents and children would sing songs and play games like hide-and-seek or tag. They loved each other so very much! Many relatives lived with the Taigi family, including a grandfather and a mother-in-law who were very mean to Anna. She cared for them with patience and Christ-like love, and treated them just as if she were serving God Himself.

One day, Jesus appeared in a vision to Anna and told her that she had a special mission from God. Her mission was to show Christians that marriage was a very holy way of life. At this time many people thought that only priests or nuns could become saints. Anna's life was to show them that married persons are also called to love and serve God with all their hearts. The Sacrament of Matrimony, by which God blesses and makes holy the love of one man and one woman for each other, is a beautiful way of living the Christian life. A holy husband and wife love one another unselfishly and show this love in the children they have. Their example reminds us that God's love lasts forever and that He shares His divine life with us, making us His adopted children.

Soon after this vision of Jesus, Anna Maria received some unusual gifts from God. She was able to heal the sick and could foretell the future. All day long, Anna could see a miraculous ball of light that was invisible to other people. This was a special "sun" in which she could see future events that were going to happen in the Church and in the world. This was not fortunetelling (which is a serious sin) but a gift from God so that she could help the Pope and other leaders during a difficult time in history. You might think that these gifts made her rich or changed her simple life. They didn't. Anna refused to accept any money for her help and always gave her attention to the needs of her family. When it was time for supper or a family outing, she would ask even very important visitors to leave her home so that the family could have time together.

After many years of such a holy Christian life, Anna Maria Taigi became very ill and died at the age of 68. She had fulfilled her mission of showing the world that the Sacrament of Matrimony is a holy and sacred way of life. Anna has been declared a Blessed of the Church which is just one step away from being an official saint. Her feastday is June 9.

The Wonder-Worker of Padua
St. Anthony of Padua — June 13

One of the most beautiful churches in all the world is in the city of Padua, Italy. Called the *Basilica of the Saint*, it is the center of devotion to one of the most popular saints who ever lived: Anthony of Padua. He is so famous that just about every Catholic church has a statue or stained glass window honoring him!

Even though Anthony is connected with Italy, he lived half of his life in Portugal, where he was born in the year 1195. His parents named him Ferdinand when he was baptized. At age 17, Ferdinand decided to become a priest and joined the Augustinian Order in his hometown. He lived in a very fancy monastery where he spent his time in prayer and study. Even as a young monk Ferdinand was *holy*, that is, full of love for God and neighbor.

One day, five enthusiastic young *friars* or members of the brand new Franciscan Order came to his monastery. They told Ferdinand how excited they were to be going as missionaries to North Africa. They were going to preach the Good News about Jesus to the Moslems who lived there. The Moslems believe in one God but not that Jesus is the very Son of God and our Savior. The Franciscans shared with Ferdinand a special secret: they hoped to be martyred for the Faith, to give up their lives so that the Moslems would come to believe the Good News. A few months later the bodies of the five missionaries returned to Portugal. They had, indeed, been martyred for the Faith! Ferdinand was now filled with only one desire: to join the Franciscan Order and be a missionary like those five young men.

The Franciscans welcomed him into their community and gave him the new name of Anthony as a sign of his new life with them. He was to be stationed in North Africa as a missionary but had to give up these plans when the ship on which he was traveling was blown off course and ended up in Italy. Anthony went to Padua in northern Italy where he joined his fellow Franciscans and was finally ordained a priest in the year 1222. He had three special gifts or talents from God that he used to spread the Catholic Faith among the people: preaching, writing, and teaching. People used to come from all over to hear Friar Anthony preach the Word of God and to ask his prayers.

God had also blessed Anthony with the gift of miracles. A *miracle* is something which can only be worked by God, who often shares this gift with his holy servants. Our Lord said that He would give this gift to His followers if their faith was deep and great. Through this gift of miracles Anthony did what Jesus had done: he cured the sick, restored life to the dead, opened blind eyes and deaf ears! He was nicknamed the *Wonder-Worker*, which many still call him today.

On June 13, 1231 Friar Anthony of Padua died. He was only 36 years old. He was so famous as a holy priest and miracle-worker that the Pope declared him to be a saint. In art, St. Anthony is usually shown holding the Child Jesus, the Bible, a loaf of bread and a lily. These remind us of the important things in his life: devotion to Christ the Son of God, to the Bible, to the needy poor, and to purity of heart and body. His feastday is June 13.

The Good Servant of Christ the King
St. Thomas More — June 22

S ome people will do anything to become rich and famous. They will even lie, cheat, and commit other sins so that they can become powerful and popular. The saint we are honoring today was just the opposite. He was already rich, famous, powerful, and popular. But he gave it all up in order to be faithful to Christ and to the holy laws of God.

ST. THOMAS

MORE ◆ MARTYR

Thomas More was born in London, England in the year 1477. This was just a few years before Columbus discovered the New World. His father was a very wealthy lawyer. Besides Tom, there were five other children in the More family. Tom was a very cheerful student who always had a smile on his face and did well in school. When he grew older he studied law at the famous Oxford University and became a lawyer just like his Dad.

When he was 27, Tom married Jane Colt. They loved each other very much and were happy to become the parents of four children. The More family lived on a beautiful estate, which is a large house with lots of outdoor space. They liked animals so much that they even had their very own backyard zoo! Thomas was very grateful to God for all that he possessed, but most of all he was thankful for being a Catholic. The Mores were a very religious family who prayed together every day. They went to Confession and Mass every week and said the family rosary before bed each night.

When Thomas was 40 the King of England, Henry VIII, made him the

79

Lord Chancellor of the nation. This was a great honor because it was the second most important position in the land. The King and Sir Thomas More (as he was now officially called) became good friends. They hunted and rode horses together. They gave advice to one another. Then something happened which would change Tom's life forever.

The King and his wife were unable to have children. This is an unfortunate thing for a king because, without children to grow up to be kings and queens, the family will lose power and leadership over the land. Henry divorced his wife and married another woman, hoping that she would give him a child. It is against God's holy law for a man and woman to divorce one another and marry someone else. Thomas knew this and so did the other citizens of the land. When the Pope reminded Henry of God's law, the King told the Holy Father to mind his own business! What a shameful thing to say to the Pope who speaks to us in Jesus' name. When his second wife failed to give him a son, King Henry divorced her, too. All together, he was married six times.

In order to do as he pleased, Henry declared himself to be the Head of the Church in England and started a new group of Protestant Christians called *Episcopalians*. He ordered all the citizens of England to join this new religion or be punished. Of course, Catholics know that only the Pope is the Head of Jesus' Church on earth. Many refused to join the new church and Thomas was one of them. This made the King very angry and he had Tom thrown into prison. The King's lawyers called Tom a traitor and sentenced him to death.

On July 6, 1535, Sir Thomas More was beheaded and became a martyr for Christ. He chose death rather than deny the holy laws of God about marriage and the leadership of the Pope. Just before dying he said to the crowd, "I am the King's good servant, but I am God's good servant first." This means that as Catholic Christians we must obey the laws of our nation but only if these laws do not go against the holy law of God. When the Pope declared Tom a saint, he also made him the patron of lawyers. We celebrate his feast every year on June 22, together with that of St. John Fisher, an English bishop who also refused to obey the King's unjust laws and was martyred like Tom.

The Voice Crying Out in the Wilderness
St. John the Baptist — June 24 and August 29

Baptism is a very old religious custom. People were being baptized even before God sent His Son, Jesus, into our world. Of course, it wasn't the Sacrament of Baptism way back then. Before Jesus came, baptism was an ordinary ceremony in which God's people showed that they wanted to be washed clean of sin.

They had to wait for the Savior to come and make baptism a sacrament that really washes away our sins and makes us children of God. The men who carried out this ordinary ceremony were called *baptists* or *baptizers*. Today's saint is the most famous of all the baptizers and prophets sent by to us by God. He was Jesus' cousin and his name was John the Baptist.

When the Virgin Mary became the Mother of Jesus, the angel told her that her relative, Elizabeth, was also going to have a baby. Mary was so happy to hear this news that she packed her things and hurried off for a three-month visit to Elizabeth's house. Upon hearing of Mary's arrival Elizabeth was filled with the Holy Spirit and cried out, "Blessed are you among women and blessed is the fruit of your womb" (*Lk 1:42*). They shared all of their special news with one another.

Elizabeth told Mary how an angel had appeared to her husband, Zechariah, telling him that she was going to have a very special baby boy named John. John was to help God's people get ready for the coming of the Messiah or Savior. Mary told Elizabeth that she, too, was visited by an angel and that the baby boy within her was the Son of God and the long-awaited Savior. Both of these holy women praised God for all the wonderful things He was doing to them for His people!

Three months after Mary arrived, Elizabeth gave birth to John. He grew up to be a fine young man filled with love for God. John left home for a while to live in the desert where he was able to spend much time in prayer and the reading of Sacred Scripture. When the time had come for him to begin his special work he started baptizing people in the Jordan River.

John became the *herald* or *forerunner* of the Messiah. In ancient times a herald or forerunner was someone who went to the various cities of a kingdom preparing the people there for the king's visit. John prepared God's people for the visit of Jesus, the King of kings. The Bible calls John "a voice crying out in the wilderness saying, 'Prepare the way of the Lord'" (*Mk 1:3*).

We learn all about John's mission in the New Testament of the Bible. The Gospels tell us that he baptized Jesus when Our Lord first started His public work among the people. These holy books also inform us of his death. It happened shortly after the Baptism of Our Lord. At that time King Herod Agrippa was living a sinful life with a woman named Herodias. He was not following God's holy law. John used to preach to the King every time he saw him and this became very embarrassing to Herodias. To please her the King finally had John arrested and thrown into prison. Soon afterwards, during Herod's birthday party, Herodias tricked him into having John killed. He ordered his soldiers to behead the Baptist and so John died as a martyr. He was about 33 years old.

St. John the Baptist has become one of the most famous and popular saints among Christians. His is mentioned by name at all Eastern Catholic Masses. Roman Catholics prepare to receive Holy Communion by listening to the words which St. John first said about Jesus, "Behold the Lamb of God Who takes away the sin of the world" (*Jn 1:29*). We celebrate two feastdays in his honor: the Birthday of St. John the Baptist on June 24, and his Martyrdom on August 29.

Did you know that there are different kinds of Catholics in the one Church started by Jesus Christ? We all believe the same teachings about God and religion. We all follow the leadership of our Holy Father. But the ways we worship at Mass and the feastdays we celebrate are different. Each of these different groups of Catholics is called a *rite*. Most belong to the *Roman Rite* and are known as *Roman Catholics*. Many others belong to the *Byzantine Rite* and are called by various names such as *Greek* or *Ukrainian Catholics*. Today we are honoring two saints who are the founders and patrons of the Church in the city of Rome. They are the holy Apostles, Peter and Paul.

St. Peter the Apostle

Peter, whose real name was Simon, was the son of a fisherman named John. His brother, St. Andrew, introduced Peter to Jesus and they both became members of the specially chosen Twelve Apostles. All four Gospels tell us more about Peter than any of the other apostles. This is because he was their leader and the leader of the whole Church after the Risen Jesus returned to Heaven.

The most important Bible story about Peter is found in the Gospel of St. Matthew. It tells us about the day that Jesus changed Simon's name to Peter (which means "rock") and made him the leader of the Church. On that day Jesus said to him, "You are Peter, and on this rock I will build My Church. I will give to you the keys to the Kingdom of Heaven" (*Mt*

16:18-19). In the language of Jesus' time, to give someone the "keys to the kingdom" meant that they were to be in charge of the kingdom and its laws. Jesus did not give this special mission just to Peter alone. He also gave it to every man who would take Peter's place as the Pope or leader of the holy Catholic Church.

After Jesus ascended into Heaven, Peter went to preach the Good News of salvation in various places. He ended up preaching in the city of Rome where he lived for the last 25 years of his life. He made Rome the center of the Church and became its first bishop. Since then the man who becomes Bishop of Rome is also the Leader or Pope of the whole Church just as Peter was.

St. Paul the Apostle

Like St. Peter, Paul also had a different name before becoming a follower of Jesus. His name was Saul and at first he was an enemy of the Christians. He used to arrest them and throw them into jail! Then one day, while he was on his way to the town of Damascus to arrest the Christians there, a bright light filled the sky and blinded Saul's eyes. The Risen Jesus appeared to him and said, "Why are you persecuting Me?" Saul asked, "Who are you, Sir?" And the Lord answered, "I am Jesus Whom you are persecuting." This taught Saul that by hurting Christians he was also hurting Jesus Himself. He was converted and received the wonderful gift of faith.

Just as Jesus had chosen the Twelve Apostles to be His helpers, so now from Heaven He chose Saul to be a helper and Apostle, too. Paul, as he was called after receiving Baptism, met with Peter to decide what he could do for Christ. He was made a bishop and spent his whole life preaching the Good News about Jesus to the Gentiles. *Gentiles* are persons who are not Jewish. At first most of the Apostles thought that only Jewish people could become Christians. Paul reminded them that Jesus died on the cross to take away the sins of all people, not just the Jews. The other Apostles agreed that this was true and made Paul the Apostle to the Gentiles. Paul is also famous for writing many Epistles or Letters which are found in the New Testament of the Bible. These letters are God's Word to us and are full of good advice for living the Christian life.

Like Peter, Paul spent the last years of his life in the great city of Rome. He had been arrested in the Holy Land and was brought to Rome for trial because he was a Roman citizen. Together with Peter, he was martyred for being an Apostle of Christ. Peter died by being crucified upside down. Paul was killed with a sword. Both of these great men of God share the same feastday of June 29. We honor them as the special helpers and protectors of the Roman Catholic Church.

The Padre and Apostle of California
Bl. Junipero Serra — July 1

Catholics have been in California for hundreds of years, even before the pilgrims landed at Plymouth Rock. They first came to the Golden State when Franciscan *Padres* or Fathers accompanied the Spanish explorers from Mexico into the beautiful lands of Baja and Alta California. While the soldiers came north looking

BL. JUNIPERRO

♦ SERRA ♦

for treasures and fame, the Padres traveled as missionaries eager to spread the Good News of Jesus among the native Indians. The greatest and holiest of these dedicated Franciscans was Blessed Junipero Serra, who is known as the *Apostle and Founder of the California Missions.*

Miguel Jose Serra was born on the Spanish island of Majorca in 1713. As a teenager he decided to become a priest and was accepted among the Franciscan Friars. It was at this time that he was named Junipero in honor of Brother Juniper, who was one of the first companions and closest friends of the Order's founder, St. Francis of Assisi. After receiving the Sacrament of Holy Orders, Junipero set sail for the New World where he served God as a missionary in Mexico for twenty years.

In 1769, 46-year-old Padre Serra volunteered to accompany an expedition of soldiers on their journey to the new and exciting territories of California. The military was going to set up a string of *presidios* or army posts in the land. Padre Serra and his brother Franciscans went with them in order to establish a chain of missions from which they could preach the Gospel among the Indians. This journey on foot from Mexico to California was very hard for Padre Serra. He had a wounded leg which never healed, yet he didn't complain about the suffering it caused him. He gladly offered this pain to Jesus for the conversion of the California natives.

During his long and often difficult years as a missionary, Padre Serra personally established nine of the twenty-one missions found in California today. The first one was built at San Diego and the last in the beautiful Carmel Valley. The missions were made up of a church, a rectory for the priests, residences and schools for Christian Indians, and plenty of land on which to farm or raise animals. The Franciscans would go out into the woods to make friends with the Indians and then invite them to the mission for catechism classes. While some of the missionaries were not as kind as they should have been, many more were good and holy men dedicated to truly helping the natives live as children of God and happy human beings. They often spoke out for the protection of the Indians against the cruelty of the local Spanish army.

It was Mission Carmel that Padre Serra chose for his home and headquarters. He lived and worked there for the last years of his life, caring for the Indians with all the love and affection of a father towards his children. During his priestly work in the missions the kind Padre baptized more than 6,000 Indians and did much to help spread the Kingdom of Christ in California.

Padre Junipero Serra died at Carmel Mission in 1784. He was 71 years old. He has always been honored as a holy man and many miracles have been granted by God through his prayers. Even government leaders recognized Padre Serra's greatness when they selected his statue to represent California at the National Statuary Hall in Washington, D.C. Our Holy Father, Pope John Paul II, spoke wonderfully of Padre Serra during his visits to California and soon after declared him a Blessed of the Church. With great joy and thanksgiving we celebrate the feast of Blessed Junipero Serra every year on July 1.

The Apostle Who Was a Twin
St. Thomas the Apostle — July 3

Have you ever found it hard to believe something fantastic that others have told you? Didn't you feel like you couldn't believe what they said unless you saw it with your very own eyes? That's exactly how today's saint felt when he first heard about the Resurrection of Jesus. He just couldn't believe that it was really true! His name was Thomas, who is often called the *Doubting Apostle*.

St. THOMAS

MY LORD AND

MY GOD

THE APOSTLE

Thomas was born in Galilee, the same part of the Holy Land that Jesus came from. We know that he was a twin because the Bible tells us that his nickname was *Didymus* which means *twin* in the Greek language. Jesus chose Thomas to become one of His Twelve Apostles. These men were Our Lord's special friends and helpers in spreading the Kingdom of God upon earth. For three years Thomas lived with Jesus and learned from Him all about the Good News of salvation.

Thomas loved Jesus with all his heart. When the Jewish leaders threatened to kill Our Lord, Thomas bravely spoke up to the other Apostles saying, "Let us also go to die with Him" (*Jn 11:16*). At the Last Supper Jesus said to Thomas these famous words about Himself, "I am the Way, the Truth, and the Life. No one comes to the Father except through Me" (*Jn 14:6*).

Thomas was not present on the first Easter Sunday night when the Risen Lord appeared to the Apostles. When the others told him that Jesus was alive and had visited with them, he refused to believe it. He said, "Unless I see the nail marks in His hands and put my hand into the wound in His side, I will not believe it" (*Jn 20:25*). A week later Jesus appeared to Thomas. He scolded him for not believing what the others had said. Jesus said to this Doubting Apostle, "Blessed are they who have not seen Me but still believe" (*Jn 20:29*).

After the coming of the Holy Spirit, Thomas went as a missionary to the land of India. He taught the people there the Good News about Jesus. Many of them believed and received the Sacrament of Baptism. Today the descendants of these first believers in India are called the *St. Thomas Christians*. Like the other Apostles Thomas died as a martyr for Christ. His feastday is celebrated every year on July 3.

The Brave Martyr for Purity
St. Maria Goretti — July 6

ST. MARIA

GORETTI

In the year 1950, a very special ceremony took place in the Vatican where the Pope lives. The Holy Father canonized a 12-year-old Italian girl named Maria Goretti. What was most unusual about this ceremony was that Maria's mother was present to celebrate the canonization. How proud Mrs. Goretti was to see the Pope and thousands of Catholics honoring her little child! But the reason Maria became a saint was not a happy event for Mrs. Goretti. She suffered a lot because of what had happened to her daughter. Here is the true story of brave Maria Goretti.

Maria was born in Ancona, Italy in 1890. The Gorettis were a poor farming family. They had seven children of whom today's saint was the oldest. When Maria was nine years old her Daddy died and she missed him very much! Mrs. Goretti now had to go to work in the fields to support her family, so Maria was put in charge of the household chores. She prayed the rosary every day asking our Blessed Mother to help her be a good girl so that life would be a bit easier for her Mom.

In her spare time, Maria would study the catechism to learn about our Catholic Faith and to prepare for her First Confession and Holy Communion. In May of 1902, Maria received both of these wonderful sacraments for the first time. She would walk several miles to the nearest church every day because she knew that the Mass is the greatest worship we can give to God. Maria also knew that receiving Holy Communion with a pure heart is the best way to grow in love for God and others. A special prayer of hers was that she would always be pure in mind, heart, and body. Although only 12, Maria looked to be 16. She was a beautiful girl with long golden-brown hair and a cheerful smile.

The weeks after her First Holy Communion rolled by as Spring turned into Summer. On a hot July day in 1902, Maria was busy working in the kitchen while everyone else was out in the fields. She heard someone enter the house. It was Alexander, a 17-year-old farm worker. Suddenly, he grabbed Maria and demanded that she disobey God's holy law about purity. He pulled out a long shining knife and threatened to kill her if she didn't do what he wanted. Maria thought quickly about Jesus dying for our sins and of how much He loves us. She bravely said to Alexander, "No! What you want to do is a sin for us. You will go to hell for it!" Filled with anger, he began stabbing poor Maria over and over again. Her screams attracted the attention of the workers out in the fields. They came running to the house and found Maria laying on the floor with bloody wounds. An ambulance was quickly called and Maria was rushed to the hospital. But it was too late. The knife wounds were so many and so deep that the doctors could not save her life. Meanwhile, the police arrested Alexander and put him in jail.

At the hospital, a priest brought Holy Communion to Maria and asked if she forgave her killer. She answered, "Yes, I forgive him and I want him to be with me in Heaven someday." This answer took a lot of love and courage! On July 2, 1902 Maria Goretti died. She was a martyr for Christian purity, reminding us how important it is to respect and honor our bodies as gifts of God.

But there is more to her story. Many years later, while Alexander was in prison, Maria appeared to him in a dream that changed his whole life. He saw her surrounded by the bright light of Heaven. She told him to be sorry for his sins and to turn to God for forgiveness. Alexander awoke and went to confession. He started to live a good Catholic Christian life and even ended up living in a monastery after being freed from jail! Alexander was also present at Maria's canonization in 1950. There, in front of thousands of people, he and Mrs. Goretti gave one another a sign of peace and forgiveness. What a heroic woman Maria's mother was... no wonder she had such a brave and holy daughter! We celebrate the life and martyrdom of St. Maria Goretti, the patroness of Catholic girls, every year on July 6.

The Saint Who Changed the World
St. Benedict — July 11

Few people realize that if it weren't for today's saint the world would be a very different place. We would not have many ancient books which teach us so much about world history. Nor would we have much of our precious music or art which has come to us because of his followers. His name is St. Benedict and

ST. BENEDICT

THE HOLY RULE OF SAINT BENEDICT

OF NURSIA

he is the founder of the great Benedictine Order that shaped the future of the Western world.

Born about 480 in Nursia, northern Italy, Benedict had a twin sister named Scholastica who also became a saint and the first Benedictine nun. When he was a youngster his wealthy parents sent Benedict to school in the city of Rome. He did very well in his studies there but was very disappointed by the sinful lives which most of the Roman people lived. At this time he also fell in love with a beautiful young lady. But Benedict felt that God was calling him to religious life not marriage. To get away from both the lady and the people's bad example, 18-year-old Benedict went to live in a monastery in the nearby hills.

The monks were glad to accept such a bright young man as Benedict. He became a *hermit*, which is someone who lives apart from everyone else and spends all his time in prayer. For three years Benedict lived this quiet life of prayer all by himself. The only person he saw or spoke with during these years was Fr. Romanus, a monk who gave him spiritual direction. Word spread about a holy hermit living in the hills, and soon many people came to ask his prayers and advice.

91

One day a group of monks came to ask Benedict to be the leader of their large monastery. He agreed but it soon became clear that he was too holy for these men. When Benedict asked them to give up some of their pleasures and comforts, many of the monks became angry with him. Some even tried to kill him by secretly poisoning his wine. But their evil plan failed when Benedict said grace before his meal and blessed the cup of wine. It shattered into many pieces! Right then and there the holy man left the monastery with a group of good monks. They were going to start a new monastery and so began the wonderful *Order of St. Benedict,* also called *Benedictines.*

Benedict wrote a special set of instructions for his monks which is now called the *Rule of St. Benedict.* It gave good advice on how to become holy through a life of prayer and work. The monks spent their days praying, chanting the Psalms, farming, copying books by hand, and designing works of art. They also gave food and clothing to the needy who came to their doors. As more and more men came to join the Benedictine Order many other monasteries were built throughout Italy. The most famous of these is Monte Cassino where Benedict lived for most of his life.

About the year 546, Benedict died while praying before the Blessed Sacrament. Over the centuries since then Benedictine monks, nuns, and laypeople (called *Oblates*) went as missionaries all over Europe, Asia, Africa, Australia, and the Americas. More than one thousand of them have become saints like their holy founder. With great joy Catholics everywhere celebrate the feast of St. Benedict every year on July 11. He is the patron of Europe and of protection against the temptations of the devil.

The Lily of the Mohawks
Bl. Kateri Tekakwitha — July 14

BL. KATERI

TEKAKWITHA

Have you ever felt left out or ignored by others? Have they ever made fun of you or told you to "go away"? If so, then you have a special friend in Heaven who knows just how horrible it feels to be treated this way by others. Perhaps she can help you learn to treat others the way that you wish they would treat you. Her name is Blessed Kateri Tekakwitha.

Tekakwitha was a Native American Indian, a member of the Mohawk tribe in the state of New York. She was born in the year 1656 to a pagan Indian father and a Catholic Indian mother. Her name in Mohawk means "she who bumps into everything." Little Tekakwitha received this name because she had very poor eyesight. He mother died when Tekakwitha was a baby so she didn't have time to have her daughter baptized and brought up as a Christian. Then her father died so she went to live with a pagan uncle who was very mean. While growing up Tekakwitha was always teased and laughed at by the other Indian girls because she was not very pretty. Yet even before she became a Catholic Christian she never tried to "get even" with the others. She never hit or made fun of them in return.

The Mohawks were a very fierce tribe. They were known for their bravery in battle and their dislike for strangers. They even killed the very first priest who had come to tell them the Good News about Jesus. Then one day, some priests who belonged to the Jesuit Order came to the

Mohawk village. They knew that the Indians might kill them, but they didn't care. Because of the color of their cassocks, the Indians called them *Blackrobes*. One of the priests told Kateri the true story of Jesus. How she loved to hear about the King and Savior of the world!

On Easter Sunday in 1676, at the age of 19, Tekakwitha received the Sacrament of Baptism which washes away original sin and makes us children of God. She also received the new Christian name of Kateri, which is Mohawk for Catherine. Being the only Catholic in her entire village was very difficult for Kateri. Now everyone really made fun of her and her new religion. They were especially mean to Kateri whenever she was praying. On Sundays, when she refused to work in obedience to God's Third Commandment, they all called her "lazy" and wouldn't let her eat at the village supper. Some of the Indians even began to hit and throw stones at her.

The Blackrobes heard of her sufferings and made a secret plan for Kateri to escape from her village. Two Catholic Indians met her one dark night outside the village. They guided her through the woods and rivers to a Christian Indian village. How happy she was to be loved and accepted by the villagers there! Kateri gave such good example of Christian purity and holiness that the people nicknamed her the *Lily of Jesus*.

Kateri spent her days in work and prayer. Everyone looked up to her as a leader and wanted to become just like her. She had a very best friend named Anastasia who also loved to pray and work. They did many things together and had such happy times! Together they went to Mass every morning and prayed the rosary every day. Kateri practiced many *virtues* or good habits like kindness, purity, patience, and helpfulness. She also knew it was important to do *penance*, which means to deny ourselves things that we like. We do penance so that we can learn self-control and become strong against temptations to sin. Since the cross is a symbol of penance Kateri always wore a necklace with a little cross on it.

Kateri had never been a very healthy person. When she was 24 years old she became very sick and was in danger of dying. Anastasia had a priest bring Holy Communion to her best friend. Afterwards Kateri said, "Jesus, I love You." Those were her last words. The villagers were very sad to hear that Kateri had died. They were sure that Jesus had taken His "Lily" to Heaven, so they prayed to her and miracles began to happen! The Blackrobes sent a message to the Holy Father saying that they thought Kateri should be made a saint. Pope John Paul II declared her a Blessed and she is the very first Native American Indian to receive this honor. We celebrate the feast of Blessed Kateri Tekakwitha in the United States on July 14.

A Mother's Gift of Love

Our Lady of Mount Carmel — July 16

OUR LADY

OF MT. CARMEL

Mothers do so many things to care for their children. They watch over us, comfort us during sad times, and teach us how to live as good Christians. The Blessed Virgin Mary is our spiritual mother. When we were baptized we became children of God the Father and brothers and sisters of Jesus. Since Mary is the Mother of Jesus she becomes our mother, too. Like a good mother she prays for us that we will be holy and happy. She has also given her children on earth a special gift from Heaven. It is called the *scapular* and it is this gift of love that we are celebrating today on the feast of Mary, Our Lady of Mount Carmel.

A long time ago, before Jesus was even born, a holy prophet named Elijah lived on Mount Carmel. This mountain is a beautiful place in the Holy Land filled with wild flowers and enjoying a breathtaking view of the sea. Elijah spent his time on Mount Carmel praying and speaking God's word to the Jewish people. Mount Carmel became known as a holy place and other men came there to live lives of prayer as Elijah had done. They especially prayed that God would send the Messiah to His people.

Ancient Christian stories tell us that after Jesus returned to Heaven, some of His followers went to preach the Good News to the holy men of Mount Carmel. They received Baptism and became hermits. A *hermit* is a monk who lives in silence and spends his days alone in prayer. The hermits had a deep love for the

Blessed Virgin and called themselves the *Brothers of Our Lady of Mount Carmel* or *Carmelites* for short. Their special work was to pray for the Church and to preach the Good News to others.

The Carmelites' peaceful life was disrupted when enemy soldiers invaded Mount Carmel. They hated Christians and killed those who would not deny the Catholic Faith. Many Brothers of Our Lady of Mount Carmel were martyred while others escaped to Europe. How sad they were to leave Mount Carmel! But the Blessed Mother did not forget about her dear Carmelites.

In the year 1251, Our Lady of Mount Carmel appeared in England to St. Simon Stock, the leader of the Carmelite Order. In one arm she held the Baby Jesus, while with the other she held out a long piece of brown cloth called a scapular. A scapular was an ancient article of clothing that was something like a long apron. It was worn over one's shoulders and hung down past the knees in both front and back. Mary told Simon that the scapular would be a reminder of her love for the Carmelites and that all who wore it would experience the help of her prayers. Simon thanked Our Lady for her gift and ordered that the scapular be worn by all the Brothers of Our Lady of Mount Carmel.

As news of Mary's gift spread, Catholics everywhere wanted to wear the scapular and receive her promise of protection and prayers. The Carmelites started a special kind of prayer group for these people called the *Confraternity of the Brown Scapular* which still has millions of members today. Many miracles have happened to those who wear the brown scapular as a sign of their love for Our Lady. The Popes of the Church have all approved this devotion to Mary and have encouraged Catholics to wear the scapular. To thank the Blessed Virgin for this mother's gift of love to her children the Church celebrates the feast of Our Lady of Mount Carmel every year on July 16.

A Woman Who Did Great Things for God

St. Bridget of Sweden — July 23

ST. BRIDGET

OF SWEDEN

Catholic visitors to the country of Sweden often find it very difficult to locate a church for Sunday Mass. The reason is because almost all of the Swedish people are Protestant Christians called *Lutherans*. It was not always this way. Hundreds of years ago Sweden was a Catholic nation and there lived in this land a wonderful and amazing saint. Her name was Brigitta (Bridget in English) and this is her story.

Before she was born in the year 1302, a holy nun had a dream about Bridget's mother. A voice in the dream said, "This woman's daughter shall do great things for God." Little Bridget was a very lively girl who loved to dance, sing, and play all kinds of games. She also enjoyed studying the catechism in order to learn all about God, Heaven, and the Catholic Christian life. Some things happened to Bridget that are most extraordinary even among the saints. When she was 10 years old the Blessed Virgin Mary appeared to her and at 12, she also experienced a vision of Jesus!

As she grew into a beautiful young woman, Bridget decided to become a nun but her father forbade it. Instead, he told her to marry Ulf Gudmarsson, who was a kind and wealthy man. Their marriage turned out to be a very happy one and they loved each other very much. Both Ulf and Bridget wanted to serve God with all their hearts, so they spent much time and money serving the sick and the poor. Their marriage was blessed with eight children, one of whom was also to become a canonized saint: Catherine of Sweden.

One day, Ulf and Bridget went on a pilgrimage. A *pilgrimage* is a religious journey. They visited many different churches and holy places in Europe. Towards the end of their pilgrimage Ulf became very ill and died. Bridget was only 39 years old at the time. Soon after this, Jesus appeared to her with an important message. He wanted Bridget to pray and work for the reform of Church and government leaders. This meant that she was to do all she could to help these leaders live better Christian lives. Bridget bravely accepted this mission and set out to do great things for God. The leaders refused to listen to her advice and most of them made fun of her. But this didn't stop Bridget from trying to carry out the mission which Jesus had given to her.

To help her better carry out this mission, Bridget and her daughter Catherine started a new religious order of monks and nuns. They called it the *Order of the Most Holy Savior.* Sister Bridget gave them the important work of praying for the conversion of all people to the holy Catholic Faith. She remembered Jesus' words at the Last Supper, "May all My followers be one... so that there may be just one flock and one shepherd" (*Jn 17:22*). This means that Jesus does not like the divisions which have separated His followers into many different kinds of Christian churches. He started just one Church, the Catholic Church, and made St. Peter the earthly leader of His followers. Jesus wants all of His followers to be members of His Church, which is the Body of Christ in the world today.

As she grew older, Sister Bridget became quite ill and had to spend most of her time in bed. But she didn't just lie there complaining! Rather, she offered up to God her many sufferings and increased her prayers for the Church and the world. On July 23, 1373 a priest celebrated Mass in her room and gave Sister Bridget her very last Holy Communion. Then she held her daughter Catherine's hand and died. Catherine went on to become the leader of the *Brigittine Order* and continued the good work which her mother had started. Several years after her death, the Pope declared Bridget a saint and made her the patroness of Sweden. We celebrate her feastday every year on July 23.

The Oldest Son of Thunder

St. James the Greater, Apostle — July 25

When Jesus chose His Twelve Apostles He included among them some who were brothers, such as Peter and Andrew, and Jude and James the Less. Another set of Apostle-brothers were James the Greater and John. It is James whom we are honoring today.

ST. JAMES

THE GREATER

James was born in Galilee and he was a fisherman along with John and their father, Zebedee. He is called *the Greater* because he was older than the other Apostle named James. Jesus gave him and John the nickname *Boanerges* which means *sons of thunder.* They were called this because they had quick tempers which Our Lord often had to help them keep under control.

One day, while James and John were busy mending their fishing nets, Jesus came walking by their boat. He invited them to become His special helpers. Right then and there, the two brothers left their fishing business and became Apostles. For three years they lived with Jesus and learned from Him the Good News of salvation. Jesus also chose James and John to become His closest companions, along with St. Peter. These three men witnessed many things in Jesus' life that even the other Apostles did not see, such as the Transfiguration on Mount Tabor and the Agony in the Garden of Olives.

Ancient Christian stories tell us that after Jesus had returned to Heaven, James the Greater brought the Good News to many places including the country of Spain. To honor his missionary journey to this land, the people built a large and beautiful shrine of St. James at Compostella, Spain. It has been a place of pilgrimage for hundreds of years. Upon returning to Jerusalem St. James the Greater became the first of the Twelve Apostles to die as a martyr for Christ. The New Testament tells us that King Herod Agrippa began persecuting the Christians in order to please certain Jewish leaders. He had James arrested and then killed by the sword.

St. James the Greater has been a favorite saint of Christians ever since the day he died. He is the patron of pilgrims and his feastday is celebrated every year on July 25.

The Sister with a Special Secret
St. Catherine Labouré — July 27

Have you ever had a wonderful secret and found it very hard to keep it all to yourself? Didn't you want to share it with others so that they could know the good news, too? The saint we are learning about today had an amazing secret which she kept all to herself for 45 years! Her name was Catherine Labouré, a Daughter of Charity who lived in Paris, France over 100 years ago.

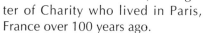

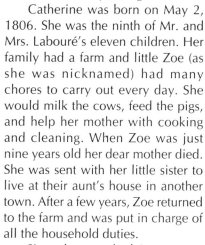

Catherine was born on May 2, 1806. She was the ninth of Mr. and Mrs. Labouré's eleven children. Her family had a farm and little Zoe (as she was nicknamed) had many chores to carry out every day. She would milk the cows, feed the pigs, and help her mother with cooking and cleaning. When Zoe was just nine years old her dear mother died. She was sent with her little sister to live at their aunt's house in another town. After a few years, Zoe returned to the farm and was put in charge of all the household duties.

Since she never had time to go to school Zoe didn't learn to read or write. But she did learn all about God and her Catholic Faith. She would begin and end each day with prayer, and when a priest was in town she would attend Mass and receive the sacraments. Zoe had a special love for Our Lady and prayed the rosary every day in her honor.

When she was 18 years old, Zoe had a dream about an old priest who asked her to come and help him serve the poor. She hadn't a clue as to who this priest could be. Later, while visiting her sister who was a nun, she saw a painting of the priest in her dream! He was St. Vincent de Paul, founder of a sisterhood called the Daughters of Charity. A few years later she entered this community and became known as Sister Catherine.

Shortly after joining the Daughters of Charity, Sister Catherine received her secret. One night, the Blessed Virgin Mary appeared to her and told her many things that would happen in the world. Our Lady stood upon a globe and had dazzling rays of light shining from her outstretched hands. Around her was written this prayer: "O Mary conceived without sin, pray for us who have recourse to you." The Blessed Virgin told Catherine that her secret mission was to have medals made that would show everyone the vision she had just seen. The Mother of Jesus said that those who wore these medals with faith in God would receive many blessings. Its purpose was to remind Christians that Mary shared in God's life of grace from the first moment of life in her mother's womb.

Sister Catherine shared this secret only with Fr. Aladel, the priest who heard her confessions. He agreed to help her carry out her mission. Soon, thousands of medals were made and were given to the Catholics of Paris. So many miracles happened to the people who wore these medals with faith that they began to call it the *miraculous medal*. No one except Fr. Aladel knew which Daughter of Charity had been chosen by Mary to give the world the miraculous medal. This was Catherine's special secret.

Over the years Sister Catherine was assigned to work with sick and elderly people in a home for the aged. She lived a quiet and busy life seeing to the many household chores that needed to be done. Towards the end of her life Our Lady gave Catherine another mission: to have a statue made which would remind everyone that Mary prays for us always. This statue showed our Blessed Mother holding a globe in her hands while her eyes were raised up towards Heaven. In order to fulfill this mission she had to tell her secret to the Sister Superior of her convent. This nun spread the secret among others. Now everyone knew the identity of the mysterious "Sister of the Miraculous Medal."

Catherine didn't mind because she knew she was soon to leave this world for Heaven. On December 31, 1876, Sister Catherine Labouré died. Thousands of people attended her funeral and thousands more traveled to Rome in 1948 to celebrate her canonization. The Daughters of Charity honor St. Catherine Labouré every year on her feastday, July 27.

102

The Soldier of Christ the King

St. Ignatius Loyola — July 31

Throughout the history of the world many men have become famous by being soldiers in the army of a powerful king. A very long time ago it was the dream of most boys to grow up to become brave soldiers, riding into battle upon some magnificent horse, and defending their kingdom against the attacks of the enemy.

ST. IGNATIUS

ALL FOR THE GREATER GLORY OF GOD. =

LOYOLA

Today's saint was one of these popular and courageous soldiers. But he ended up becoming much more famous by being a "soldier of Jesus Christ, the King of kings" in the spiritual battle of good against evil.

Ignazio (Ignatius) Loyola was born in Spain in 1491, just one year before Christopher Columbus discovered the New World. His family was very rich and his father worked for the King of Spain. There were thirteen children in the family of whom Ignatius was the youngest. As a strong teenager, he joined the King's royal army and became both a great leader and a brave soldier. Ignatius, though, was very vain about his looks and lived a rather "wild" life. Loving and obeying God were not very important to him at this time in his life.

Then one day in battle Ignatius was struck by a cannon ball! It broke his leg and brought an end to his exciting army life. He was just 30 years old. While in the hospital he had nothing to do but read, and the only book available was about the lives of the saints. At first it was boring for him, but then the stories became very interesting and exciting. He saw that the saints were something like soldiers in the battle of good against evil.

They were brave and strong in the spiritual fight for the Kingdom of God on earth. Ignatius said to himself, "If they can do it, so can I!" And from that time on he had only one goal in life: to become a saint.

He went to live by himself in a place called Manresa and there he learned all about God, prayer, and living a holy Catholic Christian life. He wrote down his thoughts in a book called the *Spiritual Exercises* and it became a favorite guide to holiness for thousands of people. Ignatius decided that God wanted him to become a priest, so he went to a seminary in Paris, France for his studies. There he met a group of very holy and dedicated men and together they started a brand new religious order: the *Society of Jesus* also called the *Jesuits*.

Ignatius wanted his Jesuits to love God with all their hearts and to help spread our holy Catholic Faith. They went to see the Pope to ask his advice about how they could best serve the Church. The Holy Father told them to preach the Good News of Jesus in every land and in every possible way. Many Jesuits became missionaries, going to the different countries of the world, and quite a few came to the New World to work among the Native Americans. To remember that they were specially dedicated to serve the Church, the Jesuits took a fourth vow of loyalty to the Pope and to his wishes for their Order.

While the other Jesuits went all over the world, St. Ignatius stayed in Rome where he set up the headquarters of the Society of Jesus. From his office he sent out priests and Brothers to build schools, start parishes, and help the poor in many ways. Ignatius himself preached in many churches and helped people grow closer to God by giving retreats. A *retreat* is a time when one goes away from his or her usual daily work to spend extra time praying and learning more about themselves and their Faith.

In the year 1556, Ignatius became ill and died. He was canonized a few years later and has become a very famous saint. The Jesuits continue his good works in every part of the world and today they are the largest group of priests and Brothers in the Church. We celebrate the feast of St. Ignatius Loyola on July 31.

The Priest Who Fought with the Devil
St. John Vianney — August 4

T he greatest thing a person can become in life is a saint. Being a saint means loving God and others more than oneself. It means doing God's will with all one's heart. You don't have to be rich, or handsome, or beautiful, or smart to become a saint. Today's saint wasn't any of these things, yet God has made him one of the holiest priests who ever lived upon this earth.

John Vianney was born in the little French village of Dardilly in 1786. He was a good and obedient boy who always tried to make his parents happy. But he wasn't very intelligent and he didn't do well in school. The other children used to make fun of him and call him names like "dummy," or even worse, "stupid." Poor John! He tried as hard as he was able but just couldn't remember his lessons.

When he was 25 years old, John decided that God wanted him to become a priest. It takes many years of study in a special college called a *seminary* before a man may be ordained to the priesthood. To everyone's surprise, John passed all of his classes even though his grades were the lowest of all the students. With God's help he made it through his studies and received the Sacrament of Holy Orders when he was 29 years old. The Bishop didn't think Fr. Vianney would do well in a big city parish, so he assigned him to a little church in the poor country parish of Ars.

Ars was a tiny village with about 230 people living in it. Fr. Vianney was shocked to learn that none of the people ever went to church. He heard that the men used bad language all day long and that the women passed many hours gossiping about others. The young pastor knew that God doesn't need priests to be smart or handsome to carry out His work. God needs holy priests, and so Fr. Vianney spent more time in prayer everyday and began to do penance for the sins of his parishioners. He begged God to convert the people of Ars into good Catholic Christians. And do you know what happened? The people did begin to change! Before long, the once empty parish church was filled with people at Mass. In the evenings many of them would gather to pray the rosary together. The parishioners of Ars even went to confession every week and soon this poor little parish became one of the best in all of France! News of the *Holy Priest of Ars*, as Fr. Vianney was now being called, spread throughout France, Italy, and other countries. People came from all over to go to confession to this wonderful pastor and to receive his priestly blessing.

About this time, Fr. Vianney began to experience strange encounters with demons. You see, the *demons*, also called *devils*, were once good angels but they refused to love and serve God. The faithful angels drove them out of Heaven and they were sent to Hell, which is the place for all those who choose to live without God in their lives. The leader of the devils is Satan, who does not want people to know, love, and serve God. He became very angry with Fr. Vianney's good work for souls and tried to scare him away from Ars. But the holy priest wasn't afraid because he knew that God is more powerful than any devil. Many times his Guardian Angel would come and chase the devils away. Soon the battle with the devil ended and I'm sure you can guess who won ... Fr. Vianney, of course!

Life and work in the little parish of Ars continued as usual for Fr. Vianney for many more years. He kept up his special prayers and penances for sinners until he was 73 years old. Then, in 1859, the holy pastor died and Catholics everywhere were sad at his passing. The Holy Father declared him a saint and made John Vianney the model and patron of all parish priests in the world. We celebrate his feast every year on August 4.

The Preacher of the Holy Rosary

St. Dominic — August 8

Do you know what the rosary is? I am sure you do because just about every Catholic in the whole world has one. Millions of people say this prayer every day. The rosary is a special prayer in honor of our Blessed Mother. We pray the rosary by reciting one Our Father, 10 Hail Marys, and one Glory Be while

ST. DOMINIC

PREACHER

thinking about certain events in the lives of Jesus and Mary. We keep count of these prayers by using a string of beads which are called *rosary beads*. Today's saint was a priest who helped make the rosary the most popular devotion among Catholic Christians.

Dominic de Guzman was born in Spain about 800 years ago. Both his mother, Isabel, and his brother, Mannes, also became saints. What a wonderful and happy family they must have been for three of them to become saints of God! Dominic was a very handsome man who received the Sacrament of Holy Orders when he was 25 years old. He was a priest in a large church where he became well-known as a talented preacher of God's holy Word.

Then one day, Dominic traveled with his bishop to the faraway land of Denmark. While on this journey they were saddened to learn about a group of people who had given up their Catholic Faith and stopped believing in the one True God. These people believed there were two gods: a good one and an evil one. They also thought that such happy things as laughing, playing, and having fun were sins!

Dominic's priestly heart was filled with love and concern for these poor confused people. He asked the bishop for permission to preach the Good News about Jesus to them so that they might live as Catholic Christians once again. Of course, the bishop gave his permission and Dominic started this new work right away. He spent many hours explaining and preaching the truth to the people but most of them didn't change. Then one night he had a dream in which the Blessed Virgin Mary told him to teach these people to pray the rosary. The very next morning Dominic did what Our Lady said and soon many of the people did begin to change. They started believing and living like Catholics once again and were so very happy!

To help him in this work of teaching others the rosary and explaining the truths of Faith, Dominic started a new religious order called the *Order of Preachers*. This order had members who were priests, brothers, nuns, and laypeople. Today the members of this order are also called *Dominicans* in honor of St. Dominic. They still preach God's Word and teach others to pray the rosary just like their holy founder did 800 years ago.

Dominic spent the rest of his life preaching the Good News and praying. He used to spend whole nights in church in the Presence of Jesus in the Blessed Sacrament. His love for Mary our Blessed Mother was also very great and he called her the Queen of his Dominican family. Dominic's faith in God was so great that God enabled him to perform wonderful miracles to help the sick and the poor.

When he was 51 years old Dominic caught a terrible fever and became very ill. In August of 1221, he died while visiting some of his Dominicans in Italy. A few years later the Holy Father declared him a saint and told his Order of Preachers to keep up the good works they were doing to spread the truth which Jesus taught us. Every year we celebrate the holy life and death of St. Dominic on August 8.

The Princess of Poverty
St. Clare of Assisi — August 11

Everyone loves to hear a magical make-believe fairy tale where the beautiful princess marries the handsome prince and they live happily ever after. The life of St. Clare of Assisi is very much like this fairy tale only better: it's true! She was a very beautiful rich young girl who met a Most Wonderful Prince and they

ST. CLARE

OF ASSISI

lived happily ever after. Can you guess Who the Prince is that Clare loved with all her heart and to Whom she gave her whole life? It is Jesus Christ, the Prince of Peace. Here is the story of how this all came to be.

Clare was born on July 16, 1193, in the Italian town of Assisi to the rich and powerful Sciffi family. She lived like a princess in a fine palace with elegant clothing and everything she wanted. But as she grew older all her fancy clothes and sparkling jewelry didn't make her happy. Deep down in her heart she felt that something was missing. Then one day, while on an outing to the marketplace, Clare saw a crowd of people gathering around a poor-looking man. He was talking to them about how much Jesus loved them and asking them to love Jesus in return with all their hearts. As Clare drew closer, she saw that the poor man was really her neighbor, Francis Bernadone. He had given up his life as a soldier and all of his money and possessions in order to serve Jesus, the King of kings. He was now called Brother Francis of Assisi, and he spent all his time preaching the Good News to others.

"How happy he looks," Clare thought to herself. And she decided right then and there to do the very same thing Francis had done. She knew her parents would never approve of such an idea, but she was now old enough to make her own decisions in life. Clare met secretly with Brother Francis and they put together a plan of action.

Late one night, while everyone was sleeping, Clare and her cousin Pacifica quietly left the palace and rode their horses to the little Chapel of Our Lady of the Angels where Brother Francis was waiting for them. Once inside, the two young women knelt before the altar and dedicated their lives to God as Sisters. They took off their fancy clothing and put on poor brown robes with ropes for belts. Brother Francis placed black veils over their heads and accepted them as the very first Sisters of his new Franciscan Order. They were called the *Poor Ladies of Assisi* but today they are known as *Poor Clares* in honor of their holy foundress.

For many years, Francis and Clare enjoyed each other's friendship and company. He would often go to visit her at the convent. After St. Francis died Clare kept reminding all of the Franciscans about their holy founder's teachings. Poverty was his most important teaching. This means that we live simple lives without a lot of "things" to get in the way of our loving and serving God. Jesus said that having lots of money and belongings makes it very hard for people to really trust in God. He said that those who were poor were specially blessed and would enter the Kingdom of Heaven.

One day, some evil soldiers tried to break into Clare's convent to harm the nuns. Quickly, Clare ran to the chapel and took the box which held the Blessed Sacrament into her hands. She went to the window, held the box up for them to see, and began to pray with all her heart. Suddenly, bright rays of light shone out from the box and the scared soldiers ran away from the convent! The nuns were safe thanks to Clare's faith in the Holy Eucharist! This is the reason why pictures of St. Clare often show her holding the Blessed Sacrament in a box or monstrance.

In 1253, after many wonderful years of serving God as a nun, Clare of Assisi died. She was declared a saint soon afterwards and in the 1950's Pope Pius XII made her the patroness of television. Of course, they didn't have T.V. way back in Clare's time. But God had given her a special gift that was something like television. When Clare was ill and confined to bed, she was still able to see Mass being celebrated in the chapel, right through the walls! The Poor Clares and all Catholics celebrate the feastday of St. Clare of Assisi every year on August 11.

Our Lady's Brave Knight
St. Maximilian Kolbe — August 14

Do you remember the Bible story about Jesus being nailed to the cross on Mt. Calvary? Did you know that when this happened He gave us Mary to be our Mother? From the cross Jesus said to the apostle John, "Behold your mother." Then He said to Mary, "Behold your son" (*Jn 19:27*). It is her mission to help each

one of us to know, love, and serve Christ her Son. The saint we are going to learn about knew how important Mary must be in our daily lives. He loved her with all his heart.

Raymond Kolbe was born in Poland in 1894. He was a very normal boy who loved to play games and pull tricks on others. One day, he did something which upset his mother very much. She said to him, "Raymond, what's ever going to become of you?" This made him sad. He didn't want to make his Mom feel bad. Raymond went to the parish church to pray to Mary, asking her for help to become a more obedient boy. Suddenly, there was a bright flash of light! Right before his eyes stood the Blessed Virgin Mary. She held out two crowns for him to see. One of them was deep red. It meant that Raymond would one day die as a martyr for Jesus. The other was shiny white. It was a sign that he would always be pure in mind, heart, and body. She said to Raymond, "Which crown do you want?" "Both!" he exclaimed. Then the vision of Mary disappeared and Raymond ran home to tell his mother what had happened.

When he was a teenager, Raymond entered the Franciscan

seminary to study for the priesthood. He received the new name of Maximilian as a sign of his new life of dedication to God. The Franciscans sent their smartest students to study in the city of Rome, Italy. Max was chosen for this honor because he was the most intelligent seminarian of them all. While he was in Rome, Max started a new group for Catholics who wanted to help teach others about Jesus and the Good News of salvation. He called this group the *Militia Immaculatae*, which is Latin for the "Knights of Mary Immaculate." It was called the M.I. for short. To join the M.I., people recited a special prayer called *Total Consecration to Mary*. They were called Knights because they fought against evil with the weapons of prayer and good example.

After starting the M.I., Max was ordained a priest and returned to Poland. He started a special Franciscan monastery called *Marytown*. This place was for priests and Brothers who were consecrated to Mary. It became the largest house of Franciscans in the whole world! Then Fr. Kolbe (as he was now called) went as a missionary to Japan. He started an M.I. monastery there, too. Life in Japan was very different than in Poland and soon Max became sick. He was called back home by his superiors and was made the leader of Marytown once again.

In 1939, a terrible war broke out in Europe. Today we call it World War II. The enemies in this war were the Nazis, who were German soldiers led by an evil man named Adolph Hitler. They were filled with hatred for God's people, both Jews and Christians, but they hated Jews the most.

They used to put them in horrible prisons called concentration camps. In 1941, Fr. Kolbe, who was filled with love for all God's people, was arrested by the Nazis. They sent him to the death camp called Auschwitz. One day, a prisoner at the camp escaped and the Nazis were furious! To get even, they chose ten men to die by starvation. When the tenth man was chosen, he started to cry out loud saying, "My poor wife and sons… I will never see them again!" Suddenly, one of the other prisoners who had not been chosen to die, stepped up to the soldier in charge. He said, "I want to die in that poor man's place." Who could this wonderful person be? It was Fr. Kolbe, Our Lady's brave Knight! The soldier agreed and Fr. Kolbe was sent with the other nine condemned men to die by starvation.

About two weeks later, on August 14, 1941, Maximilian Kolbe died as a martyr.

In 1982, Pope John Paul II declared Fr. Kolbe a saint and called him the Church's *first martyr of love*. The M.I. is now to be found all over the world with several million members. They are men, women, teenagers, and children who, trusting in the prayers and help of Mary Immaculate, want to live good Christian lives and help make our world a better place. We celebrate the feast of St. Maximilian every year on August 14.

The Angel of the Andes
St. Rose of Lima — August 23

T he country of Peru is in South America. Its largest city is Lima, which is near the great mountain chain called the Andes, and it was in this city that today's saint lived, worked, and died. Her name was Isabel de Flores but she is better known today as St. Rose of Lima.

Isabel was born on April 20, 1586. Because her cheeks were so pink and soft her parents nicknamed her Rose soon after her birth. As a little girl she learned to both read and write, which was very special for those days, and her favorite things included gardening, sewing, and singing. As she grew older, Rose also grew more beautiful. Many young men began to visit her home and wanted to marry her. But Rose had already decided what she was going to do with her life.

She wanted to be like her favorite saint, Catherine of Siena. She wanted to remain a single woman and join the Third Order of St. Dominic for laypeople. In this way she could both give herself to God and live at home to take care of her elderly parents. In those days, the Lay Dominicans often wore the special *habit* or robes of their Order. This is why pictures of St. Rose usually show her dressed up like a Sister. But really she was an ordinary young woman who earned her living by sewing clothes and selling flowers at the market.

In Lima at this time (and still today) there were many poor people who did not have enough to eat or a place to live. Rose took care of them and even set up a little hospital in her home. She used her talents to sew clothes for the poor and to buy food for the hungry. Rose did so much to help these needy people that they nicknamed her the *Angel of the Andes.* How happy she was to serve the sick and the poor just as Jesus had done when he lived on earth!

Lima is a city by the sea and it was often attacked by enemy pirates. They used to steal the gold which was in the churches of the town. Once, when a group of these English pirates was about to land at the port of Lima, Rose ran to the church in order to protect the Blessed Sacrament. When the pirates entered the church they saw Rose standing with her arms outstretched in front of the tabernacle. She was willing to die rather than let these men steal the Holy Eucharist! Without a word the thieves turned around and left Lima in peace. The whole town cheered for Rose and gave a big party in honor of her bravery.

At the same time that Rose was living and working in Lima, there were three other saints in the town. They were all friends with one another and did much to serve God and his people there. But the citizens of Lima were soon to lose their wonderful Angel of the Andes. On August 24, 1617, Rose became very ill and died. Her last words were, "Jesus, be with me." Many years later, when the Pope declared Isabel "Rose" de Flores to be a saint, she was the first person of the New World to receive this honor. We celebrate the feastday of St. Rose of Lima, patroness of all Americans, every year on August 23.

The Apostle of Honesty

St. Bartholomew, Apostle — August 24

Do you know that honesty is one of the most important *virtues* or good habits that a person can have? Nothing is so pleasing as to find a friend who is truthful and sincere. On the other hand, nothing is so disappointing as someone who is a cheater or a liar. Today's saint was praised by Jesus as being a man of honesty and truth. Because of his goodness he was chosen by Our Lord to become one of the Twelve Apostles.

Bartholomew, who is also called Nathaniel in the Bible, was born in Cana of Galilee. This was the town where Jesus worked His first miracle by changing water into wine at a wedding feast. Bartholomew was a good friend of St. Philip the Apostle. When Jesus chose Philip to become one of His special followers, Philip brought this happy news to Bartholomew. He said to him, "We have found the Messiah of whom Moses and the prophets spoke. He is Jesus the son of Joseph of Nazareth" (*Jn 1:45*). Then he invited his friend to come and meet Our Lord.

When Jesus saw Bartholomew coming towards Him He said, "Look, here comes a true Israelite. There is no dishonesty in him" (*Jn 1:47*). Bartholomew was deeply moved by meeting Our Lord. After speaking with Him for a while he proclaimed his faith in Jesus saying, "Teacher, You are the Son of God, You are the King of Israel!" (*Jn 1:49*).

When the Apostles traveled to different lands to spread the Kingdom of God, Bartholomew journeyed to

117

Armenia. He preached the Good News of salvation to the people and worked many miracles there. But, as often happens to good people, some of the Armenian leaders became jealous of his holiness. They captured Bartholomew and tortured him. He was beheaded and died as a martyr for Christ. The feast of this Apostle of honesty is celebrated every year on August 24.

The Mother Whose Prayers Were Answered

St. Monica — August 27   St. Augustine — August 28

One of the hardest things to be in life is a parent. Being married and having children is a marvelous vocation with many joys. But it also means a lot of worrying about one's children. Today we will learn of a mother who worried about her son for a long time. She cried because of his bad habits and prayed for

thirty years that he would become a Catholic Christian. God answered this mother's prayers in a wonderful way, giving even more than she had hoped to ask Him for.

Monica was born in the year 322, shortly after the Roman government stopped its persecution of Christians. She lived in the important city of Tagaste which is in North Africa. Although Monica was a Catholic Christian, her father arranged for her to marry Patricius, who was a pagan. In those days girls had to marry whomever their parents chose for them. Patricius and Monica had three children: Augustine, Navigius, and Perpetua. Patricius wouldn't allow Monica to have the children baptized, so she could only enroll them as catechumens in the Church. A *catechumen* is someone who is preparing to become a Catholic Christian. It was Augustine, her oldest child, who was to be the cause of his mother's many tears and prayers.

As Augustine grew older, Monica noticed that he was gifted in many ways but that he also had some bad habits. He was both handsome and intelligent, very popular at school, and he always earned good grades. But as a teenager he forgot about be-

119

ing a catechumen and started living a wild and sinful life. Monica worried that her son would die in his sins and lose the chance of going to Heaven forever. She did all that a mother could do to try and bring Augustine back to friendship with God. She spent a lot of time crying and praying for his conversion. When Augustine went to Rome and then to Milan where he had obtained positions as a teacher, Moncia followed him. One day, she went to speak with St. Ambrose, the holy and wise bishop of Milan. She poured out her heart to him, and his answer to her was, "Monica, a son of such tears shall never be lost." By that he meant that God would be moved by the prayers and sufferings she offered up for Augustine's conversion and grant her request.

Finally, on Easter Sunday in the year 387, Monica's long years of worrying and crying ended. Augustine gave up his sinful life and received the Sacrament of Baptism! But God had even more surprises for her. Eventually, Augustine was to become a priest, then bishop, and finally a great saint of the Church. However, Monica was to see these things from Heaven. Shortly after her son's conversion, she became very ill. One day, when she and Augustine were waiting for the ship which would take them back home to Africa, Monica said to him, "Son, I am so very happy now that you are a child of God. This is what I have spent my whole life praying for. My work here on earth is done." A few days later Monica died. She was 55 years old.

Augustine lived on for many more years. After being ordained a priest, he and a group of companions started a monastery which became very famous. Then he was consecrated as the Bishop of Hippo in North Africa and was well known for his sermons and writings about Christ and the Christian life. Augustine died in the year 430.

Both mother and son were honored by the Christians as saints and many miracles happened when people prayed to them. We celebrate their feasts on two special days: St. Monica on August 27 and St. Augustine on August 28. Monica is the patroness of Christian mothers and a good model for all who worry about and pray for their children. Augustine is the patron of those who wander from the teachings of Jesus and get caught up in sinful lives. His life shows us that we should never give up hope for those who seem very far from God. Who knows . . . they might become great saints, too!

The Mother and Servant of the Aged Poor

Bl. Jeanne Jugan — August 30

Every stage of life is a beautiful gift from God: birth, childhood, teenage years, and old age. But often elderly people are made to feel that they are a burden to their families. Sometimes, they are even abandoned by their relatives and friends. The woman whom we are going to learn about today dedicated her life to caring for elderly poor people with kindness and love.

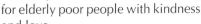

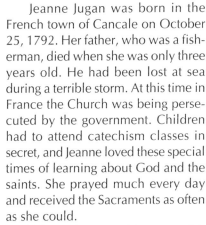

BLESSED JEANNE

The poor are our Lord Jesus Christ

♦ JUGAN ♦

Jeanne Jugan was born in the French town of Cancale on October 25, 1792. Her father, who was a fisherman, died when she was only three years old. He had been lost at sea during a terrible storm. At this time in France the Church was being persecuted by the government. Children had to attend catechism classes in secret, and Jeanne loved these special times of learning about God and the saints. She prayed much every day and received the Sacraments as often as she could.

When she was 16 years old, Jeanne became a servant in the home of a wealthy lady. Since she worked as a cook she was able to give a lot of food to the poor and the elderly of her neighborhood. Whenever someone complained about her works for the needy, Jeanne would reply, "Never forget that the poor are Our Lord." She meant that God has a special love for the poor and needy, and that any service done for them is really being done for Jesus.

In 1839, Jeanne discovered her true vocation in life. In the course of her works of charity she came upon an old woman who was abandoned and had no one to look after her. Jeanne brought this lady to her home and cared for her just as she would for Christ Himself. Together with a few friends she started the *Little Sisters of the Poor*, a new religious community of nuns devoted to the service of the elderly. When many of the poor old people of France heard of the Little Sisters, they begged Jeanne to open homes for the aged in their towns. Over the years these Sisters brought their services to the aged poor all over France, Europe and the whole world.

One day another Sister was chosen to take Jeanne's place as the superior or leader of the community. She was not very kind to Jeanne and even tried to get rid of her! But Jeanne remembered how Jesus was betrayed by His friends and how He suffered without complaining. She gave in to the leadership of the new Sister and spent the rest of her life working as an ordinary Little Sister of the Poor.

On the morning of August 29, 1879, Jeanne received the Sacrament of Anointing of the Sick. She offered a prayer to Our Lady and quietly died. She was 87 years old. On October 3, 1982, Pope John Paul II declared her to be a Blessed of the Church. This means that she will one day become an official saint. Since her death over 17,000 women have carried on her work of love as Little Sisters of the Poor. Today there are still thousands of Sisters serving the elderly all over the world. With them we celebrate the feastday of Blessed Jeanne Jugan on August 30.

The Little Girl Who Defended the Pope

St. Rose of Viterbo — September 4

ST. ROSA

You are Peter

OF VITERBO

Throughout the long history of the Church there have been many sad times for the Popes. While doing their best to carry out Jesus' command to teach and lead His followers, they have often been mistreated, teased, and even put into prison! The saint we are celebrating today loved the Holy Father with all her heart. She knew that Jesus guides us through the words of the Pope, and so she stood up for him when many Catholics were making the Holy Father suffer. Her name is St. Rose of Viterbo.

Rose was born in Viterbo, Italy in 1235. In the Italian language, her name was Rosa. She was a very good child who was blessed with great intelligence and charm. When she was eight years old, Rose caught a horrible illness and was near death. One night, the Blessed Virgin Mary appeared to her in a dream and cured her of her sickness. Our Lady told Rose that she would one day join the Third Order of St. Francis for laypeople and do many good things for the Church.

Rose did become a Lay Franciscan when she was 12 years of age. She spread the Good News of Jesus among her neighbors by her kind words and good example. She was especially fond of offering prayers and acts of penance to God to make up for the sins of those who ignored Him and His holy laws.

About this time the Emperor Frederick II and his army came to set up camp near Viterbo. He wanted to take over the Catholic Church and be the ruler of all people everywhere.

123

Little Rose was very upset by this attack upon the Holy Father and began preaching to the people of Viterbo. She reminded everyone that Jesus made St. Peter the first Pope when He said, "You are Peter, and on this rock I shall build My Church" (*Mt 16:18*). She begged her neighbors to show their faith in Christ by remaining loyal to the Pope, who takes the place of St. Peter as the leader of Christians.

Rose's father was very angry at her for preaching in public. He was afraid that the Emperor would punish her and the family because of her love for the Holy Father. Rose said to him, "Jesus suffered on the cross for me. I will be happy to suffer for Him." And suffer she did! The mayor of the town forced Rose and her parents out of the city, but the brave teenage girl kept up her preaching to the people.

Two years later the Emperor died and Rose was able to return with her family to Viterbo. She spent her days in prayer and served others by carrying out various works of mercy. On March 6, 1252, Rose of Viterbo died. She was only 17 years old. The Pope had such respect for her that he personally began the steps towards her canonization the day after her funeral. St. Rose is a good model for Catholics today who often read bad things written by those who do not respect our Holy Father. Like her we must remain faithful to the Pope and follow his leadership. The Franciscans celebrate St. Rose's feastday every year on September 4.

The Slave of the Slaves

St. Peter Claver — September 9

One of the most awful things in the history of the world was slavery. *Slavery* means that some people are owned and used by other people as things and not as human beings. Slaves were terribly mistreated and forced to do all kinds of hard work by their *masters* or owners. Black Africans were kidnapped and shipped

ST. PETER

♦ CLAVER ♦

off to North and South America as slaves. Often families were torn apart never to see one another again! Today's saint dedicated his whole life to serving and helping the poor slaves of South America. His love for them was so great that he called himself the *Slave of the slaves forever*. His name was Peter Claver.

Pedro (Peter in English) Claver was born in Spain in the year 1580. His parents were poor farmers who saved every penny they earned in order to send their son to the seminary. When he was 20 years old, Peter joined the Jesuit Order where he met a very holy man named Brother Alphonsus Rodriguez. This Brother spoke to the young seminarian about the deplorable sufferings of the slaves. He urged Peter to go to the New World to serve these unfortunate human beings. Peter was so moved by the Brother's words that he promised God he would serve the slaves for the rest of his life.

In 1610, Peter set sail for Colombia, South America. He was 30 years old. After being ordained a priest he was sent to the seaport of Cartagena where the slave ships docked on their return voyages from Africa. Most people avoided these ships because the captured slaves were sick, dying, and covered with sores. But Fr. Peter would run to the ships as soon as he heard that they had arrived. He would bring the poor frightened Africans such good things as fruit, wine, medicine, and food. The slaves could not believe that a "white" man would be so kind and loving to them! They quickly learned that Fr. Peter was their friend, doctor, and protector.

After seeing to their bodily needs, Fr. Peter would speak to the slaves about Jesus and His Good News of salvation. He knew that even though their bodies were mistreated the souls of the slaves could be free and filled with God's life of grace. They could then enjoy the happiness of Heaven forever when they died. He taught them to say this little prayer everyday, "Lord Jesus Christ, Son of God, You will be like a father and mother to me. I love You very much and I am sorry for having sinned against You." Over the years he baptized more than 30,000 slaves and consecrated each one to Our Lady.

Fr. Peter would travel to the various places where the slaves had been sent in order to celebrate Mass for them, hear confessions, and baptize their babies. Of course, he also spoke to their owners reminding them that the slaves were children of God and were to be treated with kindness. Along with many others he did what he could to try and bring an end to slavery. But it would be more than two hundred years before most of the slaves in the New World would be set free.

Fr. Peter Claver kept up his many good works on behalf of the slaves for forty years. In 1650, a horrible disease called the *plague* spread throughout the land. Fr. Peter went about nursing the sick until he, too, caught this painful illness. On the feast of Our Lady's birthday, September 8, 1654, the 71-year-old Slave of the slaves died. He was missed much by everyone, but even from Heaven he continued to help the slaves by working miracles for those who prayed to him. After many years the Pope declared Peter Claver a saint. In the United States we celebrate his feastday on September 9.

The Golden-Mouthed Preacher
St. John Chrysostom — September 13

Soon after the Resurrection of Jesus the Apostles traveled to different lands with the Good News of salvation. They baptized thousands of people and started new Christian communities wherever they went. All of these new Catholic Christians believed the same things about the Blessed Trinity, Jesus our Savior, and His

ST. JOHN

Blest are the poor in spirit

CHRYSOSTOM

holy Catholic Church. They all worshipped God by offering the holy Sacrifice of the Mass. But in the various places the people had their own special way of celebrating the Eucharist with their own kinds of prayers and songs. They began to decorate their churches differently as well.

We call these different ways of worshipping and living as Catholic Christians *rites*. There are many different rites in the Catholic Church. The two largest ones are the *Roman Rite* which comes from the city of Rome, and the *Byzantine Rite* which comes from the city of Byzantium (today it is called Istanbul in Turkey). Most Catholics in the Americas and Western Europe are Roman Catholics. Most Byzantine Catholics live in Eastern Europe, Greece, Russia, and the Mid-Eastern countries such as Israel, Lebanon and Turkey. Today's saint is very important to Byzantine Catholics. He gave them the special prayers that they use at Mass. As a matter of fact their Mass is named after him. It is called the *Liturgy of St. John Chrysostom*.

John was born in the country of Syria in the year 347. Syria is very near to the Holy Land where Jesus lived. John loved to read and did very well in school. He grew up to become a very popular teacher and lawyer. Before he became a Christian John spent much of his time at wild parties, dances, and plays with his friends. It seemed that his only goal in life was to please himself.

Then one day he met a very holy bishop who helped him to believe in Jesus. John saw how sinful and wrong his life was and he asked to be baptized. He gave up his selfish plans and decided to become a priest. When he was 39 years old, John received the Sacrament of Holy Orders. Since he had a fine talent for explaining the Word of God the archbishop made him a preacher. John was so good at it that the people soon began to call him *Chrysostom*, which in their language means "golden-mouth." How he had changed in a few years! John, who used to only please himself, now dedicated his whole life to pleasing God and serving His people, especially the poor.

When the Archbishop of Byzantium died John was chosen to take his place. What an honor this was! To be the Archbishop of Byzantium was the second most important job in the whole Church. The most important, of course, was to be the Bishop of Rome, who is the Pope and Holy Father of all Christians. At first the people cheered their new archbishop but soon they began to dislike him. You see, most of the important Christians in the city were very rich and they did not want to help those who were poor. Archbishop John reminded the rich Christians that they had a duty to take care of the poor. He preached about the *Beatitudes* which are the blessings of God which Jesus promised to those who live according to His teachings. He read many parts of the Bible where God tells us that the poor are His special friends whom He loves with all His heart. Many of the Catholics listened to their archbishop and began to help those in need. But others grew angrier and angrier at John and wanted to get rid of him.

The Queen listened to John's enemies and forced him to leave the city. He spent the last few years of his life separated from his people. Since he could no longer preach to them, he wrote about our holy Faith and his writings became very famous. Even today these writings help us to live better Christian lives. Archbishop John Chrysostom died on September 14, 407. He was 60 years old. Soon after his death he was declared a saint and the patron of preachers. We celebrate the life and work of St. John Chrysostom every year on September 13.

The Tax-Collector No One Loved
St. Matthew, Apostle — September 21

The Bible tells us that God's people, the Israelites or Jews, did not accept those whom they considered to be sinners. They especially did not like sinners called publicans. A *publican* was a tax-collector who worked for the Roman enemies of the Jews. He would take a lot of money from the people and give it to the Roman leaders. The Jewish people disliked publicans so much that they did not let them into their synagogues (churches) or homes. They would not even talk to or smile at them!

ST. MATTHEW

HOLY GOSPEL OF ST. MATTHEW +

THE APOSTLE

When Jesus came to earth He tried to change this bad attitude of God's people. He reminded us that everyone is a sinner in need of salvation. He showed us that God loves sinners even though He does not love the sins they commit. To show us how much God loves sinners, He chose a tax-collector to be one of His Twelve Apostles. This man's name was Matthew and this is his story.

Matthew, who was also called Levi, was sitting at his tax-collecting table one day when Jesus walked by. Our Lord said to him, "Come, follow Me." Do you know what Matthew did? He gave up his work right then and there and became a follower of Jesus. He was happy to meet someone who loved him and would talk to him! Matthew was so delighted that he gave a big dinner-party at his house that night in honor of his new best friend, Jesus.

Matthew invited everyone he knew to the party. Those who came were tax-collectors and other sinners. Jesus and some of His Apostles at-

129

tended the party and had a wonderful time! When the Jewish leaders heard about this they became very upset and began saying to one another, "Jesus calls himself a friend of God yet he goes to parties with sinners!" Our Lord replied, "Healthy people do not need a doctor but sick people do. I have come to bring help to sinners" (*Mt 9:12*). Jesus was reminding the leaders that sin is a like a sickness in our souls. To get rid of this sickness we need the help of our Savior, just as we need a doctor's help to heal our bodies.

Matthew loved Jesus with all his heart. He lived with Christ and the other Apostles for three years and they all became very good friends. After Jesus' Resurrection and Ascension into Heaven, Matthew and the other Apostles began preaching to the people that Jesus is the Son of God and our Savior. Matthew preached especially to the Jewish people and wrote down his memories of Christ in a gospel. "Gospel" means "good news." A *gospel* is a book written by men with the help of the Holy Spirit. It tells us what Jesus did and said when He lived upon earth.

Matthew died when he was an old man. We do not know for sure if he was martyred for the Faith like most of the other Apostles, but we think that he was. Because he was a tax-collector before becoming an Apostle, the Church honors him as the patron of bookkeepers and accountants. His feastday is September 21.

The Father of the Poor
St. Vincent de Paul — September 27

I n most Catholic parishes today there is a group of men and women who spend time every week in service to the poor and needy. They do not get paid for this work but they do it out of love for God and others. These dedicated Christians are members of a special organization called the *Society of St. Vincent de Paul.* This

Society is named after a very holy French priest who lived almost 400 years ago. This is his story.

Vincent was born in the year 1581. He had five brother and sisters. The de Paul family lived and worked on a little farm in the beautiful coun- tryside of France. Vincent loved to serve Mass and even as a little boy he wanted to become a priest. His par- ents were very happy about this and started saving up money for his semi- nary education. When he was 19 years old Vincent received the Sac- rament of Holy Orders and became a priest.

One day, while Father Vincent was travelling to another part of France, his ship was attacked by pi- rates. They captured Vincent and took him to North Africa as a slave. Since he was young and strong many people wanted to have him as their own slave. He was purchased by a Frenchman who had abandoned the Catholic Faith. While working as his slave Father Vincent prayed for the man and helped him to live as a Catholic once again. The man was so happy that he helped Vincent escape and return to France. At last he was free!

Back in France Father Vincent

had become very famous because of his adventure in North Africa. The King and Queen made him the official priest of the royal family and invited him to live in their fancy palace. But he was not happy there. Vincent had a deep love for the poor and wanted to live among them as their servant. He also wanted to preach about Jesus to others and help train men to become priests. So Father Vincent gathered together some friends and started a new religious community called the *Congregation of the Mission*. They taught in seminaries and preached in parishes. Today we call them *Vincentian Fathers and Brothers* in honor of their holy founder.

Father Vincent also started a new community of Sisters called the *Daughters of Charity*. His helper in beginning this sisterhood was St. Louise de Marillac who had been a wife and mother. With St. Louise as their leader, the Daughters of Charity served the poor by carrying out the corporal works of mercy, such as feeding the hungry and nursing the sick. One of their favorite works was to take care of orphans and other needy children. Today these Daughters of Charity of St. Vincent de Paul are the largest group of Sisters in the whole world!

There were not a lot of fantastic miracles in the life of Father Vincent like raising the dead or curing the crippled. But his many works and his religious communities are like never-ending miracles that still do much good today. His example has inspired thousands of Christians to serve the poor just as he did. St. Vincent de Paul died in the year 1660 after having spent 60 years as a dedicated priest and servant of the needy. When the Pope declared him a saint, he also made Vincent the patron of all charitable works. His feastday is September 27.

The Saint of the Roses

St. Thérèse of Lisieux — October 1

I am sure that you have seen a picture or statue of today's saint. She is dressed in brown nun's clothing and carries a crucifix surrounded by a bouquet of beautiful roses. This saint is so popular that just about every Catholic in the world knows of her. Do you know her name? It is Thérèse of the Child Jesus, but she is also nicknamed the *Little Flower*. The Popes

ST. THERESE

OF THE CHILD JESUS

have called her one of the greatest saints who ever lived. This is quite an honor because she died only 100 years ago at the young age of 24. Love for God and for others was the reason for everything she ever did. Here is her wonderful story.

Thérèse Martin was born in France on January 2, 1873. Her parents were very good Catholics and are today candidates for sainthood in the Church. Mr. and Mrs. Martin had eleven children, but only five of them lived to adulthood. Thérèse, who was the youngest, had four sisters and they loved each other very much. When she was four years old, Thérèse's mother died and her oldest sister, Pauline, took care of her like a second mother.

One day, when Thérèse was 12, she learned how prayer can help other people to love God. She read in the newspaper about a criminal who was going to be killed because of his crimes. The article also said that this man wasn't the least bit sorry for his sins. This made Thérèse very unhappy because she knew that we cannot enter Heaven if we are not sorry for our sins. So she began to pray a lot for this man, asking God to give her a sign that he was truly sorry for his crimes. Do you know what happened? On the day of his death the newspaper reported that the man suddenly had a change of heart and asked to kiss a crucifix as a sign of sorrow for his sins. How happy this made Thérèse to know that her prayers had helped to save this poor man's soul!

When she was just 15 years old, Thérèse decided to devote her whole life to helping others by becoming a Carmelite nun. The Carmelites carry out the special work of praying all day long for others. They pray that all people will know, love and serve God on earth and live with Him forever in Heaven. Sister Thérèse of the Child Jesus (as she was now called) loved her life as a Carmelite nun! She tried to do everything out of love for God and taught others to do the same. All the other nuns noticed how cheerful Sister Thérèse was and how she never complained about anything. She called this life of cheerfulness and of doing everything out of love for God her *Little Way* to holiness. She wrote all about it in a book called the *Story of A Soul*. This book is a favorite among Catholics today and it is almost as popular as the Holy Bible itself! Maybe one day you, too, will read it and learn to follow the Little Way. In it she says that she wants to spend her heaven doing good on earth.

Soon after becoming a Carmelite, Sister Thérèse caught tuberculosis, a terrible disease that attacks the lungs, and on September 30, 1897, she died. But before leaving this world for Heaven, she made a very special promise. Thérèse said that after she entered into the Kingdom of Heaven she would send roses to whoever prays to her for help. And do you know what? She really does keep her promise! Shortly following her death, a number of people said that they had received roses after having made a *novena* (nine days of prayer) to St. Thérèse. This is why she is always pictured with a bouquet of these beautiful flowers in her arms. The Pope declared Sister Thérèse to be a saint only a few short years after her death and we celebrate her feastday every year on October 1.

The Little Poor Man of Assisi
St. Francis of Assisi — October 4

ST. FRANCIS

BLEST ARE THE POOR

THE KINGDOM OF GOD IS THEIRS

OF ASSISI

Many people have special little shrines in their backyards. A *shrine* is a place where we put up a statue or picture of Jesus, Mary or one of the saints. The most popular saint for these garden shrines is Francis of Assisi. Francis had a great love and appreciation for all creation. He even wrote a beautiful song thanking God for His gifts of the sun, moon, flowers, and animals. This is one of the reasons why he has become the "backyard shrine" saint. But St. Francis of Assisi was famous for many other things, too.

He was born in the Italian town of Assisi about 800 years ago. His father was a very rich businessman who trained Francis to take over the family business. But as a strong and handsome young man, Francis wanted to become a *knight* or soldier who served in the King's army. He had lots of fun going to the parties and dances which the people gave in honor of their brave knights. During one battle Francis was captured by enemy soldiers and thrown into prison. After a little while he was released from jail and sent back to his hometown of Assisi.

One day while going for a walk in the countryside Francis came upon a leper. *Lepers* are people with a repulsive disease which destroys parts of their bodies. Most people were afraid of lepers and ran away whenever they saw one. Francis usually ran away, too. But this time something was different. Instead of running away, he embraced the leper as a sign of friendship. God blessed this brave act of love and gave Francis a change of heart. Suddenly, he lost all interest in battles and dances and parties.

While he was at Mass one day, Francis heard a reading from the Gospel of St. Matthew. It was all about giving up riches to serve the poor. Right then and there, he decided to dedicate his whole life to serving the sick and the poor out of love for God. Some other men from Assisi saw what he was doing and came to join him. Thus a new religious order of priests and Brothers came into being. They called themselves *Friars Minor* which means "Little Brothers." Francis became known as the *Little Poor Man of Assisi*. He was very popular, in part on account of the joy which never left him and in part on account of the gentle and loving way he treated others. Men came from all over to join the Little Brothers. They lived like the poorest of the poor, preaching as much through example as through words the Good News about Jesus our Savior. They also took care of the sick, the poor, and the needy. Today we call them the *Franciscans*.

St. Francis liked to pray by thinking about the sufferings of Jesus on the cross. This reminded him of how much Jesus loves us. He had a special devotion to the Blessed Virgin Mary whom he called the Queen of the Little Brothers. Francis also loved to celebrate the feastday of Christmas. It was he who started the custom of using nativity sets to honor that special night in Bethlehem when the Savior of the world was born.

As he grew older Francis became very sick and blind. He died as the sun was setting in the sky on October 3, 1226. He was 44 years old. We celebrate his feastday every year on October 4 and honor St. Francis of Assisi as the patron of ecology. *Ecology* refers to the respect and care that we take of God's gift of creation. Something special happens all over the world on the feast of St. Francis. The Franciscans invite everyone to bring their pets to church. Then they bless these animals and ask St. Francis to watch over them.

The Playboy Who Became a Saint
St. Philip Howard — October 8

Most people believe that saints were born holy. They think that these heroes and heroines of God never sinned but always did what was right. While this may be true of some saints, most of them had to work very hard at being good Christians. Today's hero was one of these not-so-good-in-the-beginning saints.

His name is St. Philip Howard, one of the many English martyrs of our Faith.

Philip was born into a royal English family in the year 1557. This was at the time in English history when it was against the law to be a Catholic in that land. Although his own Dad died as a martyr for refusing to give up his loyalty to the Pope, Philip wasn't much interested in the Catholic religion. As a matter of fact, he even became a Protestant Christian so that he would be more accepted and well-liked by the Queen. Lord Philip (as English royalty were called) was married to a lovely Protestant girl named Anne, but he spent most of his time at wild parties and dating other women! He was a playboy who thought only of pleasing himself even if it hurt other people.

One day the Queen was delighted because her soldiers had caught a very famous Jesuit priest by the name of Edmund Campion. He is now honored as a saint with his own feastday on December 1. She had him thrown into prison and sentenced to death. Just for the fun of it, Lord Philip went to hear Fr. Campion speak to his captors about the Catholic Faith. He was deeply touched by his words which made him recall his dear martyred father. Philip secretly returned to the Catholic Faith and gave up his wild life. At the same time, but unknown to her husband, Anne had also become a Catholic. How happy they both were to find out about each other!

Before long, the Queen noticed that Lord Philip no longer came to the royal parties. She sent her spies to find out what had happened to him. The spies did their work well and discovered that the Howards had become Catholics. Lord Philip was arrested and kept in prison for ten years. During this time he lived a very holy Christian life, fasting three days a week, rising every morning at 5 o'clock for prayer, and treating his captors with charity. He offered his sufferings as a penance for the many years during which he had ignored his dear wife.

In 1595, 38-year-old Philip was sentenced to death. When he asked if he could visit his wife and son the Queen answered "yes," but only if he first gave up his Catholic Faith. Bravely, Philip said "no," and so he died without ever seeing his family again. Many years later the Holy Father declared Lord Philip Howard a saint and we celebrate his feastday on October 8.

A Great Teacher of Prayer
St. Teresa of Avila — October 15

A bout 400 years ago the Catholic Church lost many of its members in Europe. During this time in history, which is called the *Protestant Reformation*, there were Catholics who stopped believing in some of the teachings of Jesus. Many of them no longer followed the leadership of the Pope. To help His Church during this difficult time, God chose a special woman who was to become a loving servant of His people. She was to help many Catholics remain faithful to Christ and His teachings. The name of this great servant was Teresa of Jesus, also called Teresa of Avila.

Teresa was born in the town of Avila in Spain in the year 1515. Her family was moderately rich and she lived a very comfortable life. As a little girl, Teresa heard a lot about Christopher Columbus and the discovery of America. As a matter of fact, three of her brothers sailed to the New World searching for treasures of gold and other riches!

When she was 13 her mother died and Teresa was sent by her father to live in a convent boarding school. Even though she was a good Christian girl, Teresa started to lose interest in God and thought more about cute boys and fancy clothes. But when she was 20 years old she began to read the Bible and decided to become a Carmelite nun!

At this time in history many nuns from rich families lived elegant lives and gave bad example to the people. At first, Sister Teresa lived an easy and carefree life like most of the other sis-

139

ters. Then one day, while she was at prayer, God spoke to Teresa. He told her to reform the Carmelite Order. *Reform* means to change things for the better. She gathered together a few sisters and they opened a new reformed convent. She was now known as Mother Teresa of Jesus.

In their new home, the Sisters lived very simple lives. They spent much time in prayer and did penance for sins. Their special work was to pray that priests would be holy and give good example to God's people. They also prayed for all those who were being drawn away from the Church and were joining the new Protestant religions. Teresa and the Sisters had many enemies who resented what they were trying to do. They were teased, laughed at, and once their convent was even set on fire! But they were brave and would not give up the work which God was asking them to do.

Over the years Teresa traveled across Spain opening up other reformed convents for nuns and for Carmelite priests, too. She also wrote many books about prayer and holiness which are still best-sellers today. Teresa reminded everyone that Christians must pray every day if they hope to truly know, love, and serve God. Without daily prayer God's life within us will not blossom and grow. God gave this good servant of the Church many special spiritual gifts like visions of Jesus, Mary, and the saints. By the end of her life, Mother Teresa of Jesus was famous throughout the land of Spain.

Her many works and travels wore her out and she became ill. On October 4, 1582, Mother Teresa of Jesus died. She left behind her a wonderful gift to the Church: the reformed Carmelites who were growing in numbers and who spread love for Jesus everywhere they went. After many years the Pope declared her a saint. In 1970, Pope Paul VI made Teresa of Jesus the very first female Doctor of the Church. A *Doctor of the Church* is a saint whose wise writings have helped Christians grow closer to God. The yearly feastday of this great servant and teacher of the Church is October 15.

The Beloved Physician
St. Luke, Evangelist — October 18

Most of the first followers of Our Lord were Jewish people who converted to Christianity. The Jewish religion began when God selected Abraham to become the spiritual father of the Chosen People who would eventually settle in the land we now know as Israel. A most important belief of the Jews was that

there was only one God and this God was going to send a *Messiah* or Savior who was to be the King and Ruler of God's people. The Israelites were very strict about who their friends were. They were especially sure not to keep company with *Gentiles* or non-Jewish people. When Jesus came into the world some of the Jews accepted Him as the promised Messiah. After His Resurrection, they became known by the word *Christians*, which means followers of Jesus Christ. The new Christians were not as strict as their Jewish leaders had been. They came to understand that God wants everyone, Jews and Gentiles, to become members of His Chosen People. He wants everyone to believe in and follow Jesus the Savior of the world.

Today's saint was one of the first Gentiles to become a Christian. His name was Luke and he was a Greek doctor whom St. Paul called the *beloved physician*. He is also thought to have been an artist who painted several *icons* or religious pictures of the Blessed Virgin Mary.

After being baptized a Christian Luke became a companion of St. Paul. Together they journeyed to various lands to spread the Good News

141

of salvation. While Paul did the preaching, Luke helped him in many ways and most probably took care of the medical needs of the people. He later wrote all about these missionary travels in a New Testament book called the *Acts of the Apostles.*

Luke was also one of the evangelists or writers of the Gospels. He recorded the many teachings of Christ as preached by St. Paul and these became known as the *Gospel of St. Luke.* This Gospel was written to remind us about God's great love for all people, especially the poor, and of His mercy towards sinners. It is from Luke's writings that we learn much about Our Lady and about the birth and childhood of Jesus. Since he was a doctor Luke has the most interesting stories about the sick people who were cured by Our Lord.

Luke stayed with St. Paul even when most others had abandoned this great Apostle during his imprisonment in Rome. After Paul's martyrdom Luke went to live in his homeland of Greece where he died at the old age of 84. He is honored as the patron of physicians and artists. We celebrate his yearly feastday on October 18.

The Bishop Who Worked Miracles
St. Anthony Claret — October 24

S ometimes people can be so silly. For example, short people, especially short men, are sometimes made to feel bad just because they aren't tall. In olden times, some people even thought that short men could not do brave things! But the Bible tells us that God judges us by what we do, not by how we look. And his-

ST. ANTHONY

CLARET

tory shows us that one's height has nothing to do with how brave a person is. Today's saint, Anthony Claret, was just over five feet tall but he became one of the most famous bishops and saints of the 19th century.

Born in Spain on December 24, 1813, Anthony was fifth of the eleven Claret children. When he was six years old he already knew that God wanted him to become a priest someday. As a young man Anthony worked as a weaver in his Dad's factory. He was so good at this trade that Anthony was known as an expert weaver by the time he was 17.

Besides his work at the factory, Anthony's daily life included morning Mass and Holy Communion, the rosary, and other prayers. He was especially devoted to the Blessed Virgin Mary and said that she had even saved his life. He had been walking along the seashore when a strong wave knocked him over and pulled him out to sea. He didn't know how to swim so he called out to our Blessed Mother for help. Suddenly, he found himself back on the sandy beach. Our Lady had worked a miracle to rescue him!

When he was 22 years old, Anthony entered the seminary and was

143

ordained a priest six years later. Father Claret loved his new life in the parish. He celebrated Mass, heard confessions, helped the poor, visited the sick, and did many other good works. The people of the parish loved him and were very happy to have Fr. Claret as their pastor. After a while, Anthony felt that God wanted him to start a new religious community. He gathered together a few friends and began this new group called the *Missionary Sons of the Immaculate Heart of Mary*. Their work was to travel wherever they were needed to preach the Good News and teach the Catholic Faith. One of their favorite undertakings was to spread devotion to the Immaculate Heart of Mary. The *Immaculate Heart* is a symbol of Our Lady's love for God and for us.

Soon after starting this new group the Pope chose Anthony to be the Archbishop of Cuba. At first Fr. Claret didn't want to accept this mission, but he obeyed the wishes of the Holy Father and set out for this faraway land. There were many people in Cuba who called themselves "Catholic" but who didn't live according to the teachings of the Church. They especially disobeyed God's laws about marriage and many men and women were living together without the blessing of the Sacrament of Matrimony. When Archbishop Claret tried to change these people, some of them hired criminals to kill him! But after a lot of work and prayers many did begin to change their sinful ways.

To help him in his mission of converting the people, God gave Archbishop Claret a marvelous gift. He was able to cure the sick with a touch from his right hand! This is why many pictures show this hand surrounded by a bright light. Along with healing the sick Anthony did many other good things for the people of Cuba like starting Catholic schools, protecting poor workers, and founding a new community of teaching Sisters. He was also a very popular author who wrote over 200 books about Christ and the Catholic Christian life.

Towards the end of his life Anthony was called back from Cuba and became chaplain to the Queen of Spain. When a revolution forced the royal family to leave the country, Anthony went with them to live in France. Then he went to Rome, Italy to attend Vatican Council I. It was this Vatican Council which reminded Catholics that the Holy Spirit keeps the Pope free from making errors when he teaches us about matters concerning Faith or Morals and living as followers of Jesus.

On October 24, 1870 Archbishop Anthony Claret died at the age of 63. He had been suffering with the disease of cancer and is now the patron saint of those who have this disease. Today, his community of priests and Brothers (called the *Claretians*) carry on his good works all over the world. We celebrate the feastday of St. Anthony Claret every year on October 24.

Two Brave Companions of Jesus
St. Simon and St. Jude — October 28

W hen Jesus chose twelve men to become the first leaders of His Church, He selected some of them from among His own relatives. One of these was Jude Thaddeus. He was a nephew of Mary and Joseph and a cousin of Jesus.

Both of his parents may be mentioned in the New Testament.

STS. JUDE & SIMON

Go out and to all preach the the world News.

APOSTLES OF JESUS

Some say that his father, Cleophas, was one of the disciples to whom the Risen Lord appeared on the road to Emmaus. And others hold that Jude's mother was the Mary who stood bravely with Our Lady at the foot of the cross on the first Good Friday. One of his brothers was also chosen to become an Apostle, James the Less. Jude's real name was Judas and this is how he is known in the New Testament. But since another Apostle by this name betrayed Jesus, Christians began to call him Jude so as not to confuse him with the traitor.

As a boy Jude must have known and played with Jesus often. As an adult he left everything in order to follow Our Lord as one of His helpers. It was at this time that he first met Simon, and Christian stories tell us that they became good friends and companions. We know very little about Simon, except that he was a devout Jew called a *Zealot*. Both Simon and Jude traveled throughout the Holy Land with Jesus and learned from the Master all about God and the Good News of salvation.

After Jesus ascended into Heaven, these two friends met together with Our lady and the other disciples. They prayed and waited for the Gift of the Holy Spirit, Whom Jesus had promised to send to all who would believe in Him. After the coming of the Spirit, Simon and Jude were filled with the missionary desire to preach the Gospel to all nations. They left Jerusalem and went to announce the Good News about Jesus to people in the land of Persia (Syria, Iraq, Iran and modern day Turkey). There were some religious leaders in that area who did not like the Apostles or their message that Jesus was the Son of God and Savior of the world. Simon and Jude suffered martyrdom at the hands of these men.

Jude Thaddeus is usually shown in art holding an image of Jesus' face. This is to remind us about an ancient Christian story about this great Apostle. One day, a powerful king fell seriously ill and asked to see Jesus, Whom he had heard to be a miracle-worker. But by the time this message reached Jerusalem, Our Lord had already been crucified and had risen from the dead. Jude knew that Jesus could still cure the king and so he volunteered to bring "Veronica's Veil" to the dying ruler. This veil was the cloth which Veronica had used to wipe Jesus' face during His carrying of the cross. In return for her kindness, Our Lord left the image of His holy face upon this veil. Upon reaching the king's palace, St. Jude blessed him with this miraculous image and the disease immediately left him!

While Simon has not become very well-known, Jude is now one of the most popular saints of the Church. He is called the *Saint of Impossible and Hopeless Cases* because he is so dear to Our Lord and his prayers are so powerful before God. Catholics throughout the world celebrate the feastday of Saints Simon and Jude on October 28.

The Brother of the Poor and Needy
St. Martin de Porres — November 3

H ave you ever seen a barber shop with its red and white pole turning 'round and 'round? Do you know why all barber shops have this unusual pole that looks like a great big candy cane? Because hundreds of years ago barbers were both hair-stylists and doctors! The pole's red color stands for blood and the white for

ST. MARTIN

What-ever you do to others

you do unto Me.

DE PORRES

bandages. Besides cutting hair these talented men set broken bones, amputated limbs, and gave out medicines to the sick. The saint we are going to learn about today became a barber-doctor when he was a teenager. He would later use this talent to serve hundreds of God's poor and needy people.

Martin de Porres was born in the city of Lima, Peru on December 9, 1579. His father was a rich Spanish soldier and his mother was a poor black servant. In those days black people were treated very badly. Martin, whose skin was dark like his mother's, was teased wherever he went. To make things worse, even his Dad was embarrassed by him, and refused to acknowledge him as his son. In fact, he abandoned the family soon after Martin was born. Poor Martin! How unfair people can be just because of skin color. But later, his Dad briefly returned and the de Porres family had a new baby sister named Juana. She loved her big brother with all her heart. She was Martin's comfort and joy.

Even as a little child Martin was special and loved God very much. He never complained about the way people treated him. Instead, he prayed for his enemies just like Jesus said we must do. He found in his Catholic Faith great comfort in hard times. Martin especially loved to pray before the tabernacle where Jesus is truly present in the Blessed Sacrament.

During his childhood Martin never wasted time feeling sorry for himself. Instead, he thought of others and would give away his clothes and food to children who were poorer than he. Once his mother had to punish him because he gave away all that the family had to eat! As a teenager, Martin learned to be a barber-doctor and was able to earn money to help others. He always divided his paycheck three ways: a lot for his Mom, a lot for the poor, and almost nothing for himself. He was a very generous young man!

When he was 15 years old, Martin decided to enter the Dominican Order. He became a Brother and took care of many chores that needed to be done in the monastery like cooking, cleaning, and some farming. Eventually he was put in charge of the infirmary, the part of the monastery where the sick members went to get well. Of course, he was their barber, too. How Brother Martin loved his new life in God's service! As a Dominican, Martin was able to do many more works for the sick and suffering people of Lima. He set up a little medical clinic for them in the infirmary of the monastery and started a soup-kitchen for the hungry, as well. He collected clothes for the naked and visited with the lonely. He remembered the teaching of Jesus that says, "Whatsoever you do to others, you do to Me" (Mt 25:40).

Martin had a special love for animals and wanted everyone to treat them kindly. One time, the Father Superior of the monastery was going to have all the mice killed because they were destroying things. Brother Martin heard word of this and ran out to the barn. He caught a mouse and said to it, "Go tell your little friends to stay away from the monastery or you all shall die." Do you know what happened? From that day on mice were never seen at Martin's monastery again!

Even though some people still made fun of Martin because of his skin color, many more came to know and love him as a special friend. When he was 60 years old, Martin caught a terrible fever and was sent to bed. On November 3, 1639 this wonderful man died while his Dominican brothers were singing a hymn to Our Lady at his bedside. Bishops came from Mexico and all over Peru to be at his funeral and to carry his casket to the grave. The people all acclaimed him as a great and holy man.

In 1962 Pope John XXIII declared Martin de Porres a saint. He is the patron of racial justice. *Racial justice* has to do with loving and treating other people fairly no matter who they are or what they look like, because everyone has been created by God our Father in His own image and likeness. Catholics everywhere celebrate the feast of St. Martin on November 3.

The Little Nun Who Did Great Big Things

St. Frances Xavier Cabrini — November 13

In the New Testament of the Bible, St. Paul tells us that God often chooses those who are weak and small to do great things for Him. He also says that we can do anything if we trust in the help of Jesus our Savior. These two Bible teachings have a lot to do with today's saint. She was weak from poor health. She was also small, barely reaching five feet tall. Many people thought that she would not be able to do much of anything, especially not great big works for God. But they were all wrong! This poor and sickly girl grew up to become the worldwide leader of a group of Missionary Sisters. She was also to become the very first United States citizen to be declared a saint!

Francesca (Frances in English) Cabrini was born in the year 1850. She had twelve brothers and sisters and they all lived on a farm in Northern Italy. The Cabrini family went to Mass every Sunday and Holy Day and received Holy Communion often. Every night before going to bed they would all gather around the fireplace to pray the family rosary. Cecca, as she was called, was very lucky because her parents enrolled her in school. In those times, many people did not think that an education was necessary for girls. She was obedient at school and studied very hard.

Francesca had always wanted to become a Sister when she grew up. But her health was so delicate that no community of nuns would accept her. When she was 22 years old, she became a teacher in an orphanage for girls. Francesca did a great job there and was much loved by almost everyone. When the Bishop heard all the good things that were said of her, he asked her to come talk with him. The Bishop wanted her to start her very own group of Sisters who would take care of children and help everyone in need. Francesca agreed and called the new community the *Missionary Sisters of the Sacred Heart of Jesus.* This happened on September 14, 1877. She now became known as Mother Cabrini.

One day, Mother Cabrini had a visit with the Pope. She had wanted to go with her Missionary Sisters to China, but the Holy Father asked her to go to the United States instead, saying, "There are many Italians who have moved with their families to America who need Italian-speaking priests and Sisters to help take care of them." Knowing that Jesus speaks to us through our Holy Father, who is His representative on earth, Mother Cabrini agreed to make the United States her special mission. She took six Sisters with her and set up her first American convent in New York. The Missionary Sisters of the Sacred Heart of Jesus then opened schools and hospitals in many other cities like Chicago, Seattle, and Los Angeles, and eventually also Denver and New Orleans.

Even though she traveled all over the world, going wherever Italians were to be found, Francesca loved America the best and became a U.S. citizen in 1914. Wherever she went, Mother Cabrini spoke to everyone about the great love which Jesus has for us. She reminded them that the Sacred Heart is a symbol of this love. She had a special way with children and one of her very favorite works was to teach them religion. She also loved to take care of poor orphans who had no family in this world. As a matter of fact, it was while she was wrapping up Christmas presents for orphans in Chicago that Mother Cabrini died on December 22, 1917. She was 67 years old.

This small and weak woman, whom everyone thought would not be able to do very much good, left behind her 1,500 Missionary Sisters who cared for the sick, the poor, and the lonely in 65 different cities of the world! Mother Cabrini was so good and holy that she was declared a saint very soon after her death. She is the patroness of all Americans who come from Italian families, and of all immigrants who leave their homeland in search of a happier life. We celebrate her feastday in the U.S.A. on November 13.

The Princess of the Poor and Sick

St. Elizabeth of Hungary — November 17

Almost every little girl likes to dress up as a princess with a fancy dress and a beautiful shining crown. Like Cinderella going to the ball, she dreams about meeting Prince Charming and living happily ever after. The life of today's saint was just like this only better…it was real life and the princess grew up to become one of Jesus' holiest followers!

In the year 1207, King Andrew and Queen Gertrude of Hungary had a beautiful baby girl whom they named Elizabeth. When she was only four years old, Princess Elizabeth was engaged to be married to little Prince Louis of Germany. In those days royal people had to marry other royal people and their families agreed to the wedding when the children were still quite young. Elizabeth grew up to become a very pretty young lady with special talents for singing and playing musical instruments. She also had a love for horses and birds, both of which she kept as pets.

When she was 14, the day for the royal wedding celebration drew near. She wore the most gorgeous gown anyone had ever seen, with lustrous jewels and sparkling diamond earrings. How proud Prince Louis felt when he saw his bride walking down the aisle of the great cathedral! And how happy Elizabeth was to see her handsome Prince! The royal couple loved each other very much and soon God blessed their marriage with three children, two boys and a girl. They had many good times together, especially at dances and other social events which Elizabeth enjoyed so much.

Louis and Elizabeth were excellent Catholics who never missed Mass and who received the Sacraments with great faith and devotion. As a princess, Elizabeth had a special concern for the needy people of her kingdom. One time she took loaves of bread from the royal kitchen and hid them in her apron so that she could sneak them out of the castle for some hungry people. Her husband, who wasn't quite as generous as his lovely wife, saw her and asked what it was that she was carrying. Legend has it that when she opened up her apron at his command, the bread had been changed into roses! God had worked this miracle to protect His dear princess and to teach her husband about the importance of serving the poor.

A few years later Prince Louis was killed in battle. Elizabeth then found out that her husband's family really didn't like her at all! They were just pretending to be friendly while the prince was alive. They forced her and the children to leave the royal castle. Elizabeth decided to dedicate her life to God and the poor as a lay member of the Franciscan Order. She started hospitals for the sick and soup kitchens for the hungry. Elizabeth never forgot that Jesus is present in the poor, the sick, and the needy. She served them with as much attention and care as she would show to Christ Himself.

Because of her close contact with the sick, Elizabeth caught a bad fever and became terribly ill. On November 17, 1231, the 24-year-old princess died after having had the joy of going to Confession and receiving Holy Communion. Only five years later the Pope declared her to be a saint and the patroness of Lay Franciscans. She is one of the married saints of the Church and a good model for husbands and wives. The yearly feastday of St. Elizabeth of Hungary is November 17.

The Bride with an Invisible Friend
St. Cecilia — November 22

A few years after Jesus rose from the dead and returned to Heaven, the Roman rulers began persecuting His followers. Christians were arrested and martyred because of their faith in Jesus. This persecution of the Church lasted for about 300 years and many famous saints were killed during this time. Several of these

ST. CECILIA

OF ROME

Roman martyrs are remembered at Mass in the First Eucharistic Prayer. Today's saint is one of them.

Cecilia was born in Rome to wealthy parents who were secret Christians. Ancient stories tell us that she was very beautiful and also very devoted to the Christian way of life. She prayed much every day and fasted often as a penance for sins. Her most special wish was to give herself to God as a consecrated virgin. This meant that she would not marry, but would spend her time in prayer and good works in the service of the Church.

But Cecilia's father had other plans for her, including marriage. Like all other girls of her time she obeyed her father's wishes and became engaged to a young man named Valerian. He was handsome, rich, and thoughtful but unfortunately not a Christian. Of course, he did not know that Cecilia and her family were secret Christians.

At her wedding party, Cecilia enjoyed the dancing and music. But in her heart she sang praise to God, trusting that He would make everything work out so that she could follow her heart's desire to live for Him alone. Suddenly, she thought about

153

her Guardian Angel and of his duty to protect her from harm. When it came time for Valerian and Cecilia to celebrate their wedding night, the beautiful bride took her new husband by the hand and said, "Valerian, you must know that I am a Christian and that I have an angel always at my side to watch over me. If you become a Christian God will give you an angel, too." Valerian did not believe Cecilia. He thought that she was just afraid of him.

Then God did something wonderful in answer to Cecilia's prayers. He allowed Valerian to see the angel, all clothed in white garments and surrounded by a bright shining light! Cecilia poured out her heart to Valerian, telling him of her secret wish to belong to Jesus alone. Generously, Valerian said "yes" to her wish. As a sign of their pure love for one another, the angel placed a crown of flowers upon their heads and then disappeared.

Soon after their wedding, Valerian was baptized and helped the persecuted Christians by burying the bodies of the martyrs. He was able to carry out this work since only a few people knew that he had been baptized. But during one of these burials Valerian was discovered by Roman soldiers and thrown into prison. Of course, he refused to give up the Faith and was martyred.

When Cecilia went to bury her husband's body, the soldiers arrested her and brought her before the judge. He knew that Cecilia's father was an important man so he was afraid of hurting her. When she refused to give up the Catholic Faith, he ordered the soldiers to take her back home and secretly kill her there. One of them took his sword and struck her in the neck three times. Thinking she was dead, the men left her house. But Cecilia was still alive although she was badly wounded. For three days she suffered and was cared for by Christian neighbors. Eventually, Cecilia died and was buried in the *catacombs*, which were underground Christian cemeteries.

The Pope and Cecilia had always been good friends. To honor her, he turned her home into a secret church and had it named after her. From the day of her death she was honored as a special saint by all the Christians in Rome. After the persecutions ended, the Holy Father had a magnificent church built on the spot where her house once stood. Because Cecilia was so joyful and sang praise to God at all times, the Church has declared her to be the patroness of musicians and singers. Pictures of this saint usually show her playing a harp or an organ. Her yearly feastday is November 22.

The Most Famous of God's Altar Boys

St. John Berchmans — November 26

For hundreds of years thousands of boys have had the honor of serving Mass. What a wonderful thing it is to help the priest as he offers to God the holy Body and Blood of Jesus Christ in the Eucharist! Did you know that most priests were altar boys when they were little? For many young men, serving at the altar is their first step in the road to the priesthood. That's how it was for today's saint who has become the most famous of God's altar boys and the patron of Mass servers everywhere. His name is St. John Berchmans.

John was born in the year 1599, in Belgium, a little country that lies between France and Holland. His father, who was the village shoemaker, was a very good Catholic and became a priest after his wife died. Young John was interested in religion and studied Latin so that he could become a priest when he grew up. He loved to serve Mass as often as he could, and prayed the rosary everyday in honor of Our Lady. As a young teenager he had two favorite hobbies: duck hunting and training dogs.

When he was 17 years old John became a novice in the Jesuit Order. A *novice* is someone who is new in a religious community. They are not full members yet but are preparing to take the vows or promises which make them members. John always tried to give good example to his fellow novices and he wrote down many of his thoughts in a journal. It is from his writings that we learn a lot about his deep love for God and others. His most famous words written in the journal were, "If I do not become a saint now when I am young, I shall never become one at all." *Sanctity* or holiness was the one great goal of his life.

In 1618, John made his vows in the Society of Jesus and was sent to Rome to continue his college education. He did so well in these studies that he was selected from among all the students to take part in a special speech competition. John was honored and he prepared very well for the event. But before it was over he had become very ill and had to drop out of the competition. The sickness turned out to be deadly and John grew weaker with each passing day.

On August 12, 1621, John asked for his three favorite things: his rosary, his crucifix, and the Rule of the Jesuit Order. He said, "These are my three treasures. With these I shall gladly die." And so he did the very next morning. He was only 22 years old. Many miracles happened at his funeral and John soon became a very popular saint. His feastday is November 26, a day that should have a special place in the heart of altar boys everywhere.

The Fisherman Who Was Chosen First

St. Andrew, Apostle — November 30

Most people like to be chosen first to be on a team. There seems to be something special about being picked before anyone else. It is an honor which we all enjoy. Today's saint was the very first man to be chosen by Jesus to become one of His special disciples or followers. His name was Andrew of Galilee.

ST. ANDREW

Jesus said "I will make you fishers of men."

THE APOSTLE

Andrew was born in the little town of Bethsaida in the land of Galilee, close to Nazareth where Jesus lived as a boy. His father was John the fisherman and his mother was named Joanna. Andrew's brother was Simon who later became known as the Apostle Peter, leader of the first Christians. As a little boy, Andrew used to go fishing with his Dad and when he grew up both he and Peter decided to become fishermen, too.

Andrew loved God with all his heart and waited for the coming of the promised Messiah or Savior. He became friends with St. John the Baptist, who was preparing God's people for the coming of the Messiah. One day, while he was visiting with John, Jesus came walking by. Suddenly, John pointed to Our Lord and cried out, "Look! There is the Lamb of God who takes away the sins of the world!" This meant that Jesus was the promised Savior. Andrew went after Our Lord and spent a few hours talking with Him. Then Jesus said to Andrew, "Come, follow Me." This is how he became the very first of the special followers of Christ.

Andrew was so happy and excited about Jesus that he ran home to tell Peter all about Our Lord. He said to his brother, "I have found the Messiah!" Peter went to meet Jesus and became a disciple, too. Soon after this, while the two brothers were fishing, Jesus came to them and said, "I will make you fishers of men" (*Mk 1:17*). This meant that they would bring many people to God by their preaching of the Good News and by baptizing new Christians.

During the three years of Jesus' work among God's people, Andrew was one of the Twelve Apostles who lived with Our Lord. He listened carefully to Christ's teachings and did whatever Jesus said. Do you remember the Bible story about the loaves and fishes? It was Andrew who found the little boy in the crowd who had the basket of bread and fish that Jesus blessed and multiplied.

After the Resurrection of Jesus, Andrew met together with Our Lady and the other followers of Christ in Jerusalem. They prayed for the Gift of the Holy Spirit, Who came to them on the great feast of Pentecost. An ancient Christian story tells us that it was Andrew who asked the Apostle John to write down his memories of Jesus. These writings became known as the *Gospel of St. John*. When the Twelve Apostles decided to travel throughout the world to spread the Good News about Jesus, Andrew went to preach to the people of Russia and Greece. While he was in the country of Greece, Andrew converted the wife of Ageas, who was the governor of the land. This upset Ageas very much so he ordered his soldiers to arrest and kill Andrew. They tied him to an "X" shaped cross but he did not die right away. For two whole days Andrew continued to preach about Jesus. Then he died as a martyr for Christ.

The name "Andrew" means "brave" and it was a good name for this Apostle. He did many brave things to teach others about Jesus. Catholics and other Christians honor St. Andrew every year on his feastday of November 30. He is the patron saint of fishermen, and of the lands of Russia, Scotland, and Greece. St. Andrew is also a good model for brothers in a family since he loved his own brother very much and helped him to become a follower of Jesus.

The World's Greatest Missionary
St. Francis Xavier — December 3

J ust before Jesus returned to Heaven He said to His Apostles, "Go out into the whole world and preach the Gospel to all people. He who believes and is baptized will be saved, but he who does not believe will be condemned" (*Mk 16:15-16*). These words of Our Lord are His commandment to us to spread the Good News of salvation to others, especially to those who are not Christians. This spreading of the Gospel is called the *missionary work* of the Church. All Christians, no matter who they are or what they do, are called by Jesus to be His *missionaries* in the world. Some people devote their whole lives to this work by joining missionary groups as priests, Sisters, Brothers, or laypeople. Today's saint was one of these dedicated persons. His name is Francis Xavier and he is called the world's greatest missionary.

Francis was born on April 17, 1502, in the Basque region of Spain. His parents were very wealthy and they desired a rich and successful life for Francis, their sixth and youngest child. So when he was a teenager he went off to study law at the University of Paris. Francis soon became one of the most popular students at the school. He earned very good grades and was excellent at sports, especially in track and high-jumping. On top of all this, Francis was very vain about wearing only fancy clothes and having a perfect appearance.

One day a new student came to the university and was assigned as Francis' roommate. His name was Ignatius Loyola. Ignatius was twice as

ST. FRANCIS

◆ XAVIER ◆

159

old as Francis and much more serious about living a good Christian life. The two did not get along well at first, but the older Loyola was a good influence for the rich young Xavier. Slowly but surely Francis began to change his ways. After many months he even decided to join Ignatius and a few other men in starting a new religious order called the *Society of Jesus* or *Jesuits* on August 15, 1534.

Soon afterwards Francis was ordained a priest and was filled with one burning desire: to bring the Good News of Jesus those who had never heard about Our Lord. On April 17, 1541, Francis' dream came true when he set sail as a missionary for the land of India. Upon arrival in this foreign country Francis immediately began his missionary work by visiting prisons, caring for the sick in hospitals, and teaching catechism. He was a very talented preacher who converted many to the Catholic Faith.

After working in India Francis' love for souls urged him on to preach the Gospel in other lands. He went to Ceylon, Malaysia, and finally Japan. He was the very first European to set foot in Kyoto, then the royal capital of Japan. The Emperor was so impressed by Fr. Xavier that he allowed him to preach the Good News throughout the nation. As his work in Japan was drawing to a close, Francis made plans to set up a mission in China. But this was not meant to be.

Francis' work and busy life made him weak and he caught a deadly fever. On December 3, 1552, he died while quietly repeating the Holy Name of Jesus. He was 46 years old and had baptized about 50,000 new Catholic Christians during his eleven years as a missionary. Seventy years later the Holy Father proclaimed him a saint and he became the patron of the missionary work of the Church. His feastday is celebrated with great joy all over the world every year on December 3.

The Saint Who Became Santa Claus
St. Nicholas — December 6

I n some countries of the world Catholic children celebrate December 6 with great joy! It is the feast of St. Nicholas, patron of children, giver of gifts, and the saint who has become known as Santa Claus! On the night before this special day, the children place their shoes at the doors of their homes. When they awake in the morning, those who have been kind and obedient during the past year find their shoes stuffed with candy and little presents. Naughty children find a black lump of coal! Who was this holy man who is so loved by both children and adults alike?

Nicholas was born in the land of Asia Minor (modern day Turkey) around the year 280. He was an only child who was educated by an uncle who was a bishop. When he was 19 years old, Nicholas received the Sacrament of Holy Orders by which Our Lord calls men to serve Him as priests. Father Nicholas had a talent for preaching the Word of God and he became very popular among the Catholic people. He was also well known because of his deep love for God and others.

In the year 303, the Roman Emperor Diocletian ordered his soldiers to burn down all Christian churches. All the holy books for Mass were to be destroyed and the priests arrested! Nicholas was imprisoned and beaten by his cruel captors. After a while a new emperor came into power and Nicholas was freed from jail.

Not long after his release from prison, Nicholas was chosen to become the new bishop of the diocese

161

of Myra. At this time in history many Christians were confused about their faith. They weren't sure if Jesus was really the Son of God. They thought that He was just a very good man who did great things for God. Bishop Nicholas spent a lot of his time preaching the truth about Christ to these people. He reminded them that our Savior was truly God the Son, Who came to us from Heaven and was born of the Blessed Virgin Mary.

Nicholas, like all of God's saints, had a tender love for the sick, the poor, and the needy. There are many stories about his care of the poor. The story from which part of the Santa Claus legend comes tells us that there was a father who had three daughters. They were so poor that no man would even think about marrying any one of them! When Nicholas heard this he became very sad. He thought up a secret plan to help them. Late one dark night, while most of the town was asleep, Nicholas quietly went to this family's house and threw three bags of money through an open window. Imagine the delight which filled the daughters' hearts when they awoke to find such wonderful surprise gifts!

Nicholas, however, didn't become a saint because he gave gifts to the needy. One becomes a saint by doing everything for the love of God and by showing this love in generous service to others. When he died, the people of Myra were very sad but they knew that their holy bishop had gone to Heaven. Ever since his death many miracles have happened for those who ask his prayers and he has become one of the most popular saints among *Byzantine* or Eastern Rite Christians. St. Nicholas is the patron of Russia and Greece, countries where thousands of boys and girls receive some form of his name at Baptism.

Now that you know a bit about Nicholas' life, you can see how he became the model for Santa Claus. Besides borrowing our saint's name, Santa also is said to bring surprise gifts during the night and to stuff stockings with lots of goodies. He even wears red and white which are the traditional colors of St. Nicholas' robes. The real Jolly Old St. Nicholas is still honored by many boys and girls. He prays to Jesus for them everyday, especially on his feastday of December 6.

The Aztec and the Queen of the New World
Bl. Juan Diego — December 9
Our Lady of Guadalupe — December 12

The arrival of the Spanish *conquistadors* or conquerors in Mexico in the 16th century was both bad and good news for the native Aztec people. It was bad news because so many of them were mistreated, tortured, or killed by the soldiers. But there was good news, too, because the Spanish priests who came as missionaries preached the Gospel of Jesus to the natives and freed them from their cruel Aztec religion. This religion was very bloody and even included human sacrifices! Today we are honoring a very holy Aztec man and we are celebrating the visions of Mary, *Our Lady of Guadalupe*, who chose this man to be a missionary of Jesus among the native Indians.

One of the converts of the missionaries was a poor Aztec named Juan Diego. He and his wife, Maria Lucia, loved God with all their hearts and lived good Catholic lives among their pagan Aztec neighbors in the village of Tolpetlac. After his wife died, Juan spent more time at church and took care of his sick uncle, Juan Bernadino. He used to walk to Mass in nearby Mexico City everyday and it was during one of these walks that Our Lady chose him to be her special messenger.

On the morning of December 9, 1531, as Juan was on his way to Mass to celebrate the feast of the Immaculate Conception of Mary, he heard a strange but sweet voice call his name. Looking up he noticed a mysterious light shining from the top of nearby Mount Tepeyac. As he drew nearer to the light, Juan saw within it a young

163

woman dressed like an Aztec princess. She had dark hair and a most beautiful face. The Princess was dressed in a fancy pink gown covered with golden threads and wore a soft blue veil which was decorated with stars. She was standing upon a silver crescent moon and had her hands folded in prayer, worshipping the one True God who had sent her. Juan Diego fell to his knees before this lovely Lady. She spoke to him saying, "I am the Ever-Virgin Mary, Mother of the True God. I wish a church to be built here so that I can show my love for all the people of this land. Go and tell the Bishop all that you have seen and heard."

Eager to carry out the command of his Heavenly Queen, Juan ran all the way to the Bishop's house in Mexico City. He told the Bishop all about the Beautiful Lady and of her wish that a church be built upon Mount Tepeyac. Sadly, the Bishop did not believe a word he said and sent Juan Diego away. The Lady was waiting for him as he returned to Tepeyac. She said, "Do not be sad. Go in peace to your village and return to the Bishop tomorrow morning. Tell him again that the Mother of God wishes a church to be built here."

Before sunrise the next morning Juan set out for Mexico City. Again the Bishop refused to believe him. But he did ask Juan to bring him a sign to prove that his story was true. Upon reaching Tepeyac the Blessed Virgin greeted Juan with kindness and thanked him for being obedient and patient. She asked him to return in the morning and promised to give him the sign which the Bishop desired. Filled with joy at this promise Juan hurried back to his village. Upon entering his home he was saddened to find his uncle, Juan Bernadino, very ill and at the point of death. The next day he missed his appointment with Our Lady so that he could care for his dear uncle, who was growing weaker with each passing hour.

Early on the morning of Tuesday, December 12, Juan decided to run to Mexico City in order to ask a priest to bring the sacraments to Juan Bernadino. To avoid being delayed by Our Lady he took a different path to the city, bypassing Mount Tepeyac. But the Mother of God knew his plans and appeared to him anyway! Juan felt embarrassed because he had tried to avoid her. She said to him, "Where are you going, my little son? Don't you know that I would never forget to help those who love me? Do not worry about your uncle, he is cured of his sickness as we speak. Now climb up to the top of

Tepeyac and there you will find roses. Cut and place them in your *tilma* (cloak) and bring these flowers to the Bishop. Tell him that it is Our Lady of Guadalupe who sends him this sign." Juan knew that no roses grew upon Tepeyac, especially not in December! But there upon the mountain top, as far as the eye could see, was a wonderful garden of gorgeous Roses of Castile in full bloom! He obeyed Our Lady's instructions and placed the flowers inside the folds of his tilma.

Upon reaching the church in Mexico City, Juan burst into the Bishop's office. He opened up his tilma and the roses fell to the floor. But the Bishop paid no attention to the beautiful flowers. Instead, he and the priests looked at Juan's cloak and fell to their knees. For there upon his poor tilma the Virgin had left a miraculous picture of herself just as she looked in her appearances to Juan Diego! The Bishop begged Juan's forgiveness for not believing his story and ordered a church to be built upon Tepeyac right away. He took Juan's tilma, had it framed, and placed it in the new Shrine of Our Lady of Guadalupe after it had been built. It can still be seen today, 460 years later, as fresh and marvelous as it was that day when Juan first brought his rose-filled tilma to the Bishop.

In the years after the apparitions Juan Diego spent his days taking care of the shrine and writing down the story of Our Lady of Guadalupe. Because of Mary's heavenly visits to Tepeyac and Juan's obedience to her words millions of Aztecs converted to the Faith and so Mexico became a great Catholic country. The Virgin of Guadalupe was proclaimed the Queen of the New World and Juan Diego was honored as her special messenger. Not long ago the Holy Father declared him a Blessed of the Church and a model of evangelization. *Evangelization* means doing all that we can by our good example and kind words to prepare people's hearts to welcome Jesus as their Lord and Savior. Catholics of the Americas retell the story of Blessed Juan Diego and celebrate the feast of Our Lady of Guadalupe with great joy every year on December 12.

Do you remember the story of St. Agatha, *The Brave Girl of Sicily*? Today's saint was very much like Agatha, in fact, she lived at about the same time and in the same place. Her name is Lucy and she was a brave martyr, too.

Lucy was born about the year 285 in the town of Syracuse, Sic-

ST. LUCY

SANTA LUCIA

ily. Her father died when she was little, leaving the family very wealthy. As a teenager Lucy wanted to dedicate herself totally to God just as St. Agatha had done. Her mother, however, had very different plans for her daughter. She wanted Lucy to marry and had even chosen the young man who was to be her future husband.

Lucy was able to change her mother's mind during a pilgrimage they made to the shrine of St. Agatha. Her mother was suffering from an incurable disease and Lucy suggested that they go to the shrine of the brave martyr to ask God for a cure. It was decided that if God cured the mother through the prayers of St. Agatha, Lucy would be free to follow her heart's desire of belonging to God alone. While praying at the shrine her mother was cured, and she, too, decided to dedicate the rest of her life to God! Both of them gave their wealth away to the poor and took up lives of prayer and service to God's people.

The man who was to have married Lucy became furious when he heard this news. He reported Lucy to the police for being a secret Christian. Since it was against the law to be a follower of Jesus Christ, Lucy was arrested and thrown into prison. The soldiers tortured her and tried to make her give up her faith in Jesus. Of course, Lucy would not betray Our Lord. To make her suffer for this choice, her captors injured her eyes and then killed her with a sword. This happened in the year 304, when Lucy was 19 years old.

The Christians honored Lucy as a martyr-saint and she soon became as popular as St. Agatha. Because of her suffering she is often pictured holding a plate of eyes and is the patroness of those with eye trouble. St. Lucy's name means *light* and since her feastday is celebrated during the Advent season she reminds us to prepare for the coming of Christ, the Light of the world. In Sweden there is a wonderful Advent custom in her honor called the *Santa Lucia*. On her feastday of December 13, young girls dress in special Santa Lucia costumes and serve breakfast to their families. This reminds us that Lucy had dedicated her life to serving others.

The Christmas Companions of Christ
St. Stephen—December 26   St. John the Apostle—December 27
The Holy Innocents — December 28

CHRISTMAS

GOS-
PEL
OF

ST.
JOHN

COMPANIONS

For over 1,500 years it has been a Catholic custom to celebrate three special feastdays of saints right after Christmas Day. These saints are called the *Christmas Companions of Christ* and are meant to remind us that the greatest gift we can offer God is the gift of our lives in martyrdom. *Martyrdom* is the giving up of our lives in order to remain faithful to Jesus and His Catholic Church. There are three groups or kinds of martyrs: those who knowingly die for Jesus, those who suffer persecution for their faith in Jesus, and those who are killed for Jesus even though they are unaware of it (such as little children or those who are severely mentally retarded). These special Christmas saints are Stephen, John the Apostle, and the Holy Innocents of Bethlehem.

St. Stephen — December 26

Stephen's story is found in the New Testament book called the *Acts of the Apostles.* He was a young Jewish convert to Christianity who became the first deacon of the Church. A *deacon* is a man who receives the Sacrament of Holy Orders but does not become a priest. His work is to serve the needy and to assist bishops and priests in the celebration of the Mass and Sacraments. The Bible tells us that Stephen was filled with God's grace and worked many miracles among the people. He had a special gift for preaching the Word of God in a clear and interesting way.

One day, the Jewish leaders asked Stephen to speak to them about his new faith. They grew furious when he said that Jesus was the Son of God and the promised Messiah. They began to yell at Stephen and some of them dragged him outside the city gates. While he knelt in prayer and continued his preaching, the angry men threw large sharp stones at him and killed the brave young deacon. Stephen died forgiving his enemies and asking God to forgive them, too. This happened in the year 34, just a few months after Jesus had risen from the dead. Stephen was the very first Christian martyr.

St. John the Apostle — December 27

When Jesus began His mission of preaching the Good News among God's people, He chose twelve men to become His closest friends and helpers. John was a teenager when he became one of these Twelve Apostles along with his older brother, James. Together with Peter and James, John became one of the closest companions of Jesus. He became Jesus' best friend and was nicknamed the *disciple whom Jesus loved*. You can read all about him in the Gospels.

After Our Lord's crucifixion and Resurrection, John took care of our Blessed Mother. He wrote one of the Gospels and several of the Letters of the New Testament. In all of these sacred writings, John reminds us that God is love, and that love is the greatest commandment of God. For this reason he is often called the *Apostle of Divine Love*.

When he was old, John was arrested by Roman soldiers and thrown into prison. They beat him and made him suffer in many ways because of his faith in Jesus. The governor was going to have him killed, but at the last minute he changed his mind. Instead, he ordered John to leave the country never to return. For this reason John is honored as a martyr, but he died from natural causes when he was about 94 years old. He was the last of the Twelve Apostles of the Lord to leave this world.

The Holy Innocents — December 28

The Gospel of St. Matthew tells us that King Herod became very jealous and angry when the Three Kings came looking for the Baby Jesus, the newborn King of the Jews. Herod did not want there to be another king, so he ordered his soldiers to go to the little town of Bethlehem. They were to kill all baby boys who were two years old or younger! By ordering this horrible slaughter Herod thought that he would do away with Jesus and remain the only King of the Jews.

But, as we all know, the Baby Jesus was not killed. An angel of the Lord appeared to Joseph in a dream and told him to escape with Mary and the Christ Child. Joseph awoke and immediately obeyed the will of God. After many days of travel, the Holy Family arrived safely in the land of Egypt. A few years later they would return to their homeland and settle in the town of Nazareth.

But in Bethlehem the cries of mothers and fathers could be heard throughout the streets. The soldiers had cruelly killed all of their little boys because of Herod's hatred for Jesus. We honor these little boys of Bethlehem and call them the *Holy Innocents*. They are holy because they died for Jesus as martyrs. They are known as innocents because they did nothing wrong and were killed simply because of one awful man's jealousy and hatred.

Index of Names